AF285853

Fürderer
Option and Component Bundling under Demand Risk

GABLER EDITION WISSENSCHAFT

Ralph Fürderer

Option and Component Bundling under Demand Risk

Mass Customization Strategies in the Automobile Industry

With a Foreword
by Prof. Dr. Arnd Huchzermeier

Springer Fachmedien Wiesbaden GmbH

Die Deutsche Bibliothek - CIP-Einheitsaufnahme

Fürderer, Ralph:
Option and component bundling under demand risk : mass
customization strategies in the automobile industry
/ Ralph Fürderer. With a foreword by Arnd Huchzermeier.
(Gabler Edition Wissenschaft)
Zugl.: Koblenz, Wiss. Hochsch. für Unternehmensführung, Diss., 1995
ISBN 978-3-8244-6279-7   ISBN 978-3-663-08818-9 (eBook)
DOI 10.1007/978-3-663-08818-9

© Springer Fachmedien Wiesbaden 1996
Ursprünglich erschienen bei Betriebswirtschaftlicher Verlag Dr. Th. Gabler GmbH, Wiesbaden 1996
Lektorat: Claudia Splittgerber

Das Werk einschließlich aller seiner Teile ist urheberrechtlich geschützt.
Jede Verwertung außerhalb der engen Grenzen des Urheberrechts-
gesetzes ist ohne Zustimmung des Verlages unzulässig und strafbar. Das
gilt insbesondere für Vervielfältigungen, Übersetzungen, Mikroverfil-
mungen und die Einspeicherung und Verarbeitung in elektronischen
Systemen.

Höchste inhaltliche und technische Qualität unserer Produkte ist unser Ziel. Bei der Produktion und
Auslieferung unserer Bücher wollen wir die Umwelt schonen: Dieses Buch ist auf säurefreiem und
chlorfrei gebleichtem Papier gedruckt.

Die Wiedergabe von Gebrauchsnamen, Handelsnamen, Warenbezeichnungen usw. in diesem
Werk berechtigt auch ohne besondere Kennzeichnung nicht zu der Annahme, daß solche Namen
im Sinne der Warenzeichen- und Markenschutz-Gesetzgebung als frei zu betrachten wären
und daher von jedermann benutzt werden dürften.

ISBN 978-3-8244-6279-7

Foreword

In today's world, customers, not firms, are the driving force behind product variety and speed of innovation. Increased global competition and the opening of newly developed markets raise the pressure even further. High margins for newly developed products are short-lived and thus these products become quickly commodity items. The cash-flow generated by the new product is required for the financing of the research and the development activities of the next generation of products. Successful firms do take the lead in this vicious cycle and do not release products prematurely; the unsuccessful ones launch products late and, as a result, often do not generate sufficient capital required.

Ralph Fürderer explicitly addresses the cross-functional tradeoff in the implementation of mass customization strategies. In practice the debate looms between Marketing who wants to broaden product variety and Manufacturing who needs to lower overall costs. Alternatively, the practice of product bundling and bundle pricing can be deployed effectively and thus lead to the best of both worlds, i.e., lower costs, higher prices and higher expected sales through increased service levels!

The main managerial insight is that products need to be tailored to the customer's reservation prices or willingness to pay for individual product features and options. Thus, there is no need to fulfill all customer requirements. From a manufacturing point of view, the products need to be tailored, too. Scale effects through modular design of components enhance the ease of assembly and foster the quick response capability for customized or bundled products. For this reason advanced planning of component designs and assembly lines prior to the market launch poses the greatest challenge for manufacturing planning. Ralph Fürderer addresses this complex planning problem in this book. However, the potential benefits - as demonstrated in this book - can be rather rewarding.

This book provides an excellent integration of the different aspects of manufacturing and marketing planning. Moreover, the methods have been implemented and the results have been validated at Adam Opel AG. My colleague, Professor Linus E. Schrage, from the Graduate School of Business of the University of Chicago, and I consider this work an outstanding contribution to the theory and practice of world class manufacturing management. The concepts described in this book have been integrated already in the curricula of leading Business Schools throughout the world.

Prof. Dr. Arnd Huchzermeier

Preface

In times of quickly growing technical complexity, heterogeneous needs in competitive sales markets, and substantial demand uncertainty due to lead times in Planning, the task of increasing the profitability of a car manufacturer's product line requires powerful decision support systems.

The work presents an integrative framework of the Product Engineering and Manufacturing side in terms of product costs and variant driven complexity costs, as well as the sales revenues on the Marketing side, determined by the stochastic structure of demand and competition. The proposed mathematical optimization models for the system component design and the stochastic price bundling are of large scale in practice, and some can not be solved by traditional local search approaches. We have therefore developed and analyzed new solution algorithms which account for the inherent data complexity and non-concavity.

Moreover, the work reports of the implementation of the presented methods at a world-class car producer using efficient data collection methods for empirical validation on real car concept problems. Due to the versatility of the approach, its application is not limited to production industries.

Many people have played important roles in the development of this book. As a non-economist, my views on Operations Research were greatly influenced by the excellent teachers I have had. Professor Arnd Huchzermeier accompanied me during the entire project providing "engines, brakes and safety belts" in many difficult situations. I have benefited a great deal from his ideas and the ideal way of supervision. To Professor Linus E. Schrage and Professor R. Kipp Martin at the University of Chicago, I not only owe a lot of good suggestions and thorough paper revisions, but also the invaluable disclosure of many exciting facets of OR beyond the scope of this book.

As a non-engineer, at the Adam Opel AG I learned what it takes to build a car and to sell it. In particular, I would like to thank Hans-Joachim Gora, Dr. Eckhard Dornauf and Heinrich Zapf for their support during my time at the Vehicle Computation Department.

Many thanks also go to Dr. Andreas Herrmann for his valuable comments and for always having an open door.

Last not least, I want to thank Petra for her love and patience. During many months, she frequently had to put up with a boarder who ignored laundry, communication, and sunny Sunday afternoons for the sake of getting this work accomplished.

Ralph Fürderer

Contents

List of Figures

Chapter 1

Introduction

Since the era of Henry Ford's legendary Model T, all attempts to sell a standard
world car have proven to be unsuccessful. Paying tribute to customers individualism
and heterogeneous preferences, car producers have substantially increased their product variety in the last twenty years. Technology advances have made manufacturing
tools and processes more flexible to allow for a quick response to changing demand.
Through early integration of the three C's Computer Aided Design (CAD), Engineering (CAE) and Manufacturing (CAM), the development time for a new car model
has been cut down to under four years. Dense dealer networks and advanced logistics
have shortened customer order lead time to approximately two weeks. Therefore,
a car producer can afford to vary the standard equipment of one car model depending on the socio-cultural, geographic or climatic needs of different target markets.
Moreover, the manufacturer has to meet country specific legal and environmental
requirements, such as emission, noise or lighting standards. The customization of
a car model is achieved by additionally offering a set of customer-determined options, so-called free-flow options, such as air-conditioning, sun-roof, metallic exterior
colors, leather trim, alloy wheels and so forth, in line with entire equipment packages. The extent of free-flow option and package supply should depend on the target
market and its customers budget constraints.

As most world class car producers have reached a comparable level of technical

sophistication and quality, the cutting edge is the ability to manage the issues of
product variety: what type of variety should be offered, in which quantities and
how can it be produced at least cost. Even in the age of lean manufacturing and
system modularity, today's car is still put together by several thousands of different
parts or functional components. Free-flow options cause rapid growth of production
specific car variants. Associated with many options, option combinations, and thus
car variants are volume dependent variable costs as well as variant dependent fix
costs, e.g., development costs, administrative costs or logistic costs.

Current strategies for controlling proliferation costs aim at either an increase of manufacturing process flexibility, or development of product designs which allow for
variety accommodation measures, such as part commonality or component modularity. Design and functionality of almost all build components, as car body, door
modules, wiring harnesses, struts etc., depend on the car's option content or a particular subset of options. Whereas the design of a battery is only determined by a few
options in terms of their power consumption and its physical size, a very complex
functional component such as the wiring harness depends on all electrical options.
Dividing a harness which serves n dashboard options and m body options into a
dashboard and a body module, reduces the number of potential designs from 2^{n+m}
to $2^n + 2^m$. But for a typical size of n, m of 20, this still results in an infeasible
number of designs, since a car manufacturer can not store thousands of harnesses
of different option contents at the assembly line. On the other hand, it may be
uneconomic to have too few types of a component with the resulting need to over-
design them: reducing the number of different batteries to only one in the limit
case would mean to equip each car with a maximum capacity battery. In general,
increasing product costs can not be passed to the customer in form of higher prices
and thus may outweigh cost savings through deproliferation by far. A cost optimal
approach is a tradeoff which thoroughly balances market and manufacturing constraints. The need for analytical decision support models in product development
can not be denied (Ulrich, 1993). Spreadsheet based optimization or "what if" analyses will become as inevitable tools for the design engineers as CAD and CAE based
technical product development systems.

The "you name it - we build it" strategy is indeed a misunderstanding of mass customization practices and is also contrasted with actual purchase and option selection behavior. Experience shows that demand is limited to a small fraction of all possible car variants which can theoretically be ordered by the customer. However, technical development of components, planning facility layout and tool design, or production readiness of the suppliers require considerable lead times. Most far-reaching decisions have to be made many months before actual consumer choice behavior can be observed. In the first part of this work, we present a mathematical model, employing stochastic programming, to determine the optimal number of designs and the design specifications of any build component to minimize marginal costs under demand uncertainty. For this purpose, we need a detailed description of the sales volume for future car types. This information is usually not available on a disaggregated level. We show, how to generate such a future car pool by merging car sale history with single option forecasts, utilizing a straightforward linear programming approach.

In many car segments, brand loyalty is higher than 80%. Hence, a car manufacturer does not exclusively seek to minimize his costs as a reaction to some given market scenarios. He must furthermore give leverage to his ability to identify the needs of individual customer segments and increase his profit avoiding the risk of losing former customers or not attracting new customers. An important tool for seizing markets is a car's equipment supply.

In general, there are two extreme car sales practices with regard to variety management of equipment supply. Asian manufacturers, producing cars for their overseas markets in Europe and America for instance, limit their offer to six or seven major options which results in less than a hundred production and customer specific car variants. Long transportation lead times do not allow for a competitive make-to-order business policy, hence safety stocks of different car variants have to be built up in economic sizes in the destination country. Moreover, few car variants substantially reduce opportunity and logistics costs. However, they strictly confine the customers individual choices. To avoid this market disadvantage, many options can be postponed by the customer and are subsequently installed by the dealer. A manufacturer, targeting his products for his regional market, does not want to give up his lead-time advantage and do without a part of his vital option business. He may employ the strategy mentioned above to offer a wide variety of free flow options -

mostly with considerable cost disadvantages. A widespread practice to profit from
economies of scope, product enhancement and demand stimulation is option bundling, in form of equipment packages or special car editions. In the second part of
our work, we suggest a mixed integer nonlinear programming method to optimize
bundle composition and bundle prices in view of profit, if customer demand and
choice behavior is uncertain.

In this work, we address three key problems of today's car producers: the timing
issue (management needs to make production decisions today), the demand issue
(markets are unpredictable), and the pricing issue (markets have different tastes).
The following roadmap will show how the thesis is organized.

1.1   Roadmap

The thesis can be separated into two parts. In the first part, we deal with the
management of technical complexity. The central question is how to design components, such as exhaust systems, wiring harnesses or batteries which do not impact
demand as long as the cars overall functionality is not affected. The cost minimization problem is motivated in section 2.1, and we give a comprehensive review of
problem-related literature in section 2.2. Since a global view of costs is essential for
a successful system component design strategy, the main cost drivers are analyzed
and eventually aggregated to an overall cost function including product costs as well
as complexity costs in section 2.3. In section 2.4, we address the problem of demand
uncertainty. We introduce a mathematical model which allows to combine detailed
current sales information with aggregated market performance forecasts of certain
car equipment patterns. The cost optimization will then be built upon the resulting
projected vehicle data base. The stochastic optimization model itself is formulated in section 2.5. Solving this problem means to determine the optimal component
designs and their number in order to minimize overall costs, if a set of demand scenarios with certain assigned probabilities is employed. Efficient solution techniques of
this mixed linear integer problem are very difficult to find because the number of
constraints is quickly increasing. We analyze three solution methods in section 2.6

and furthermore comment on the general tractability of the optimization problem. In section 2.7, the solution methods are benchmarked with regard to randomly generated car data as well as with regard to real data from the European automobile industry. The chapter is concluded with a summary in section 2.8. In the second part, shift our point of view from mere technical complexity to customer specific variety and the problem of mass customization. The crucial question is, what is the profit maximizing variety of equipment a car producer should offer with his base cars and which customization strategy should be deployed. For this reason, we motivate the classical problem of product bundling and bundle pricing in our automotive framework in section 3.1 and review the essential literature in section 3.2. The branch specific aspects of bundling, such as the impact on complexity, potential sales strategies and so forth, are presented in section 3.3. A mathematical model is set up in section 3.4 which for the first time allows to find the optimal tradeoff between total costs and revenue for several customization strategies, if demand is uncertain. Since the resulting mixed non-linear integer optimization problem is very complicated and only locally solvable, some new tools from mathematical homotopy and bifurcation theory are introduced and utilized. Moreover, we show how to efficiently collect the necessary input data. In section 3.5, we present a heuristic solution method for the stochastic bundling problem based on decomposition. Again, we use real car data to assess strengths and weaknesses of our method and translate our numerous numerical experiments into implementable management guidelines in section 3.6. The presented work on this issue is wrapped up in section 3.7. Comments and ideas on possible research extensions are given in chapter 4.

Chapter 2

Cost Optimization of System Components

2.1 Motivation

Functionality and design of many subsystems, particularly chassis and electrical components, depend on the employment of some characteristic options in a car model. The major conflict is whether to build a "one-size-fits-all" component which is capable to handle the entire range of product requirements or to tailor alternative product designs. Inevitable for such a product planning problem is a well suited cost structure which allows to consider variant and volume driven costs. We illustrate this crucial optimization problem for a wiring harness module which is probably one of the most complex assemblies in a car. The presented method, however, is not component specific and can thus be applied to any other component or product. In addition, we carry out a cost optimization of car batteries.

A wiring harness can be regarded as a bundle of pre-assembled electrical cables with plugs or relays at each end. The cables are designed to either connect a power consuming device with another one (like, for instance, the central airbag sensor with the airbag ignition and inflation device), or directly link a power consuming device to a power source (interior lights, air conditioning). A car usually consists of several wiring harness modules that drive the engine/transmission system, instrument panel functions, electric doors and body options. In general, these modules are mutually independent in functionality.

To illustrate the significance of wiring harness design and manufacturing, consider the following data on the currently produced V-car model of the Adam Opel AG. The Opel Omega can be regarded as a typical passenger car of the upper size car segment:

- A customer can freely order about 40 electrical options, e.g., engine size, transmission (manual, automatic), passenger airbag, cruise control, anti-theft system, electric sun-roof/air conditioning, and so forth. A large number of electrical options is already contained in the standard package, e.g., driver air-bag, anti-lock brakes (ABS), radio/CD-player, multi-functional display, and so forth.

- The total number of currently used wiring harnesses in production is 150 with approximately 1,250 wires each.

- The overall length of wires per car equals 2,200 meters.

- The number of connectors, plugs, and terminals of all wiring harnesses in the car amounts to about 2,100.

- Almost 55% of all walk-home-failures (this term is used to illustrate how the driver gets back home) are due to electrical problems.

- Electric components contribute to 20% of the car's value.

The three major issues in wiring harness manufacturing clearly can be identified as managing complexity, quality and costs which are strongly interrelated. We will not consider quality issues in this paper.

The challenge for the car producer is now to develop an "optimal" wiring policy which has to be set up 18-24 months **before** production actually starts. The most important constraint, that must never be violated, is that each car in production must get exactly one wiring harness which serves all of the particular car's specific electrical options. Due to the inevitable uncertainty of consumer preferences which predict the demand for a car with a certain option configuration, this policy has to be very robust and flexible towards potential demand fluctuations. Thus, a certain amount of so-called "mandatory" harnesses, designed for the highest equipment levels of a car, have to be included in each policy. They ensure, that the above feasibility constraint is never jeopardized which would cause essential delays in meeting the customer delivery lead time.

Obviously, there exist two extreme wiring strategies: with regard to the combinatorial option explosion one could suggest only to install mandatory harnesses. But, to do without additional harnesses is a very costly approach. Leanly equipped cars will get a high-grade harness, a lot of option content in terms of material is given away, and this in turn means increased marginal costs.

The second alternative is the genuine just-in-time approach: each car gets exactly the wiring harness that it actually needs, without any waste of content. In view of the fact that cars with a low option content sum up to a high volume, they must be taken into consideration. Hence, this strategy means quickly increasing fix costs due to storage and administration activities (see section 2.3) for the car producer, who has not yet achieved perfect production leanness. One lean "vision", for instance, is to implement a Supply-In-Line-Sequence system (SILS). In perfection, this means that the option requirements of a vehicle on the assembly line is transmitted by an on-line system to the supplier, shortly before the wiring harness has to be installed in the car. Instead of buffering inventory or delivering harnesses in larger batches, supplier and manufacturer maintain a continuous pipeline delivery system which is highly responsive and flexible. But even manufacturers such as NUMMI with highly sophisticated logistics and a small number of different car variants due to option packages instead of free-flow options, cannot even afford to share the high infra-structural costs for SILS-techniques with their suppliers.

Traditionally, world car manufacturers have been polarized between both approaches: NUMMI, Toyota and a couple of other Japanese producers share the first philosophy: reduce proliferation and only store a little number of harnesses, accepting a certain amount of wasted money. Most European and American companies such as VW, Fiat, Ford, and so forth, store a huge number of harness types at the assembly line, to avoid of installing too "generous" harnesses, but for the bane of their fix costs (for a more detailed description see Fuerderer, 1994). Considering both concepts, there clearly is a need for a tradeoff: the strategy must be to identify similar car types with respect to their option content, group them and design the most inexpensive harness for the entire group. Figure 2.1 shows a characteristic overall cost behavior, depending on the number of content-optimized harnesses or number of groups of similar car types: for a low number of harnesses the determining cost factor clearly is variable. Increasing this number means to provide better tailored cables, producing at lower costs. For a very high number of harnesses, the marginal benefit of a new harness is less than the additional fix costs. Somewhere in between, one encounters a global cost minimum. The range of potential numbers of harnesses

Figure 2.1: Typical Harness Cost Function

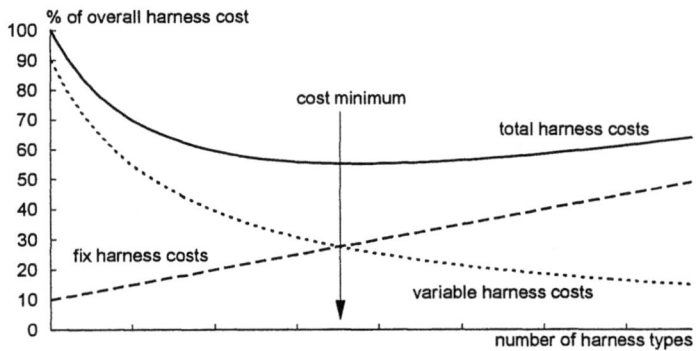

is strictly limited in practice: a lower bound is the number of mandatory harnesses which ensure the feasibility of a harness policy, the upper bound is due to storage capacity, handling restrictions or other complexity limits.

The main contribution of this chapter is to classify and to conduct a thorough analysis of the mathematical structure of the problem. We suggest a stochastic mathematical formulation of the cost optimization of system components (COSYC) and to provide a heuristic algorithm to optimally design wiring harnesses, long before actual demand can be observed. Once a vehicle is produced according to order forecasts, updates of the initial production plan based on actual orders are necessary to raise the firm's profitability.

In section 2.2, we give a comprehensive review of the related literature. The cost structure and deproliferation impact is assessed in section 2.3. In section 2.4 we show how to obtain a "micro"-forecast for future car types, broken down to the option level. We use current sales figures, the new product definitions and all available option forecasts to set up a linear program which can be used with standard linear programming software tools. This disaggregated car scenario not only serves as an important base case for the COSYC problem, but also provides valuable information for marketing and strategic planning. The COSYC problem is formulated as a stochastic integer program in section 2.5, and we present a heuristic solution method, based on decomposition. For this purpose, we use a genetic-type algorithm, embedded in a greedy procedure. Alternative solution strategies, i.e., column generation or B&B will be discussed in section 2.6 as well. We employ real data for a large car manufacturer to conduct a cost optimization of wiring harnesses, steering columns and batteries in section 2.7, and we conclude with a summary in section 2.8.

2.2 Literature Review

In the sparse literature concerned with wire harnesses, the major contribution comes from electrical engineering. The main concerns of the manufacturing side can be roughly divided into three topics: process cost computation (Ong, 1993), process control (Singh, 1987) or harness testing (Anderson, 1982). As one sees, these subjects exclusively cover the process side rather than the planning side and do not address wiring harness cost reduction issues by design modularity.

In spite of the lack of direct links to the literature, one encounters well-known problem settings which may be called "related" to the COSYC problem. These approaches share the same basic ideas identify similar objects, group them and find a cost-minimum cover in terms of a precisely defined objective. We will consider three major problem types:

- Packing or Cutting problems.

- Set Covering/Partitioning problems.

- Facility Location problems.

Geometrical interpretations of the COSYC on one side make one think of a packing problem which could be briefly described as the task to choose a set of one to three dimensional objects, in order to optimally package or cover smaller items. Another interpretation may lead to set covering or set partitioning problems: for a given family of sets find a cost-optimal cover or partitioning. These two problem classes, their applications and relations to the COSYC will be extensively considered in the following sections. The last problem setting discussed at this stage is probably the one with the closest link to the COSYC problem and is mainly referred to as Location/Allocation Planning Problem, where one needs to decide where to locate a new plant given a set of already existing facilities. A fixed amount of costs needs to be paid for each new plant opened, variable costs arise from the transportation of goods. The Allocation part forces the manager to think of explicit groupings of existing facilities (customers) which will be served by new plants in a cost optimal way. This approach is very strongly related to the idea of grouping car types appropriately and to design the cost optimal harnesses for each group of "similar" car types.

2.2.1   Packing Problems

In practice, packing, filling, loading or cutting problems have to be dealt with. Consider the task of filling a large object of a given size and shape with smaller objects of some size and shape in such a way to achieve an optimal fill rate with respect to a well determined objective. A large part of these problems arise from a geometrical background, thus usually restricted to two or three dimensions. Nevertheless, we find a couple of non-geometrical problems which can be formally described as a packing or cutting problem. In many cases, the work done on these problems is motivated by practical settings and the constraints may be quite specific.

Variations of the packing and cutting problems can be encountered in areas as varied as computing and publishing to shipping and construction. In the construction industry, long steel bars need to be cut in smaller pieces of specific lengths to serve as structural reinforcements. A similar problem from radiator manufacturing is to cut tubes for heat units. These one-dimensional and less complicated problems can be solved by a variety of efficient methods.

In the paper industry, the raw paper is manufactured in wide rolls, called *tambours*. Each tambour later has to be cut lengthwise into smaller rolls, called *finals*, where the radii of the cylindrical finals usually are smaller than the tambour radius. Thus, a tambour will be used for multiple cutting procedures. The question how to decide on the different tambour widths is often called *assortment stock problem*. The *trim loss* or *cutting stock problem* asks for a cutting procedure which suits the demand of several finals for given tambour widths. An other variant of this two-dimensional problem arises in the textile industry where a standard shape of cloth needs to be cut in irregular pieces.

The problem of, for instance, cutting rectangles into smaller ones can be found in the steel, glass, furniture, plywood and wallpaper industry, while the constraints may vary: in glass industry cuts of large screens need to go from one edge to the other, called *guillotine cuts*, while in furniture or plywood industry the cutting objective is to avoid any defects in raw material. For a comprehensive review of application-oriented research see Sweeney and Paternoster (1992).

Other well-known problems with geometrical background are: the *pallet loading problem* from materials handling, where a unit load for safe and efficient transportation has to be constructed (Hodgson, 1982; Ram, 1992); the *bucking problem*, where a felled tree is cut into shorter logs which are later sawn into lumber (Faaland and

Briggs, 1984; Pnevmaticos and Mann, 1973). A three-dimensional packing problem is that of filling containers (trucks, ships, cargo airplane) with smaller objects of some shape, or storing stock in a warehouse (Gardner, 1979).

That some problems of non-geometrical nature can be derived from geometrical settings, can be demonstrated with the two-dimensional *bin-packing problem*, where a number of small bins with fixed extensions need to be placed in a minimum number of larger bins. A related non-geometrical problem is the job scheduling on computers. The memory and time required for each job is a given, and the problem is to schedule the jobs in a way to minimize the overall execution time. The width of the bin or rectangle is taken to represent the available memory and their height to represent time. Another related problem is the *assembly line balancing problem* (Wee & Magazine, 1982), where the tact times or workstation capacities are the equivalent of the bins. The smaller items are the durations of several jobs or tasks that have to be accomplished. For that purpose, NUMMI has set up a "common sense algorithm" in form of a Gantt-chart-type magnetic wall in each working section where the tact time corresponds to the height of a sketched rectangle. Each job is represented by a small metal plate, whose height corresponds to the task duration. Jobs can be balanced by reordering the plates or assigning them to other workstations focusing on critical paths. In order to arrive at a feasible solution however, the order in which these jobs need to be executed, has to be considered. Except for these precedence constraints, the logical structure of the line balancing problem is the same as that for the classical bin-packing problem.

An interesting application of the packing problem to *multiprocessor scheduling* was considered by Coffman, Garey and Johnson (1978): Given a set $T = \{t_1, \ldots, t_n\}$ of tasks, each task t_i having length $l(t_i)$, and a set of $m \geq 2$ identical processors. A schedule is a partition $\mathcal{P} = (P_j)_{j=1}^{m}$ of T into m disjoint sets, one for each processor. The j-th processor executes all tasks in P_j. Tasks are assumed to be independent, so that there need not to be any idle time between consecutive tasks. The sequence in which tasks are executed is, by the same reason, irrelevant to the problem. The finishing time for a schedule $\mathcal{P}$ is defined as

$$f(\mathcal{P}) \;=\; \max_{1 \leq j \leq m} \sum_{i \in P_j} l(t_i) \quad, \tag{2.1}$$

where $l(p_j)$ is defined as the sum of all single task lengths which form p_j. The optimum m-processor schedule $\mathcal{P}^*$ is the one that satisfies

$$f(\mathcal{P}^*) \;=\; \min\{f(\mathcal{P}) \mid \mathcal{P} \text{ partition of } \mathcal{T}\} \quad . \tag{2.2}$$

The problem of finding the optimum schedule is known to be NP-complete (Ullman, 1976), (see section 2.2.3).

Other problems with geometrical links are: the *change making problem* (Martello and Toth, 1980), where a cashier has to assemble a given amount of change using the minimum number of coins; the *capital budgeting problem* (Lorie and Savage, 1955), or the traditional *knapsack problem* (Dantzig, 1957; Martello and Toth, 1990), where a wanderer needs to fill his knapsack with value and weight assigned items, in order to maximize the overall value of the filling, where a given overall weight must not be exceeded.

The majority of recently examined cutting or packing problems is of two- or three dimensional nature (Sweeney and Paternoster, 1992). Formulations of the problem however can be stated independently of problem dimensions.

Objective

$$\min \sum_{j=1}^{m} \sum_{i=1}^{s_j} c_{ij} \cdot x_{ij} \quad , \tag{2.3}$$

subject to

$$\sum_{j=1}^{m} \sum_{i=1}^{s_j} a_{kij} \cdot x_{ij} = r_k \quad k = 1, \ldots, n \quad , \tag{2.4}$$

$$\sum_{i=1}^{s_j} x_{ij} \leq w_j \quad j = 1, \ldots, m \quad , \tag{2.5}$$

$$x_{ij} \geq 0 \;, \text{ integer}, \quad i = 1, \ldots, s_j, \, j = 1, \ldots, m \quad , \tag{2.6}$$

where

$n \;=\;$ the quantity of types of objects.

$k \;=\; 1 \ldots n.$

$r_k \;=\;$ the quantity of type k objects.

m =   the quantity of types of containers.

j = $1 \ldots m$

w_j =   the quantity of type j containers available.

s_j =   the quantity of packing patterns for container type k.

i = $1 \ldots s_j$.

x_{ij} =   the quantity of type j containers using pattern i.

c_{ij} =   cost of packing pattern i of container j.

a_{kij} =   the quantity of type k objects in container type j using packing pattern i.

x_{ij} =   the quantity of type j containers using pattern i.

The objective (2.3) clearly is to minimize packing costs. Constraint (2.4) ensures that each object k is actually packed, whereas constraint (2.5) limits the capacity of each container j.

As for the COSYC, in most cases it is not possible to explicitly consider all packing patterns. Instead, mathematical algorithms are used to generate feasible patterns which mostly are obtained by solving a corresponding subproblem (e.g. column generation). In practice, these methods are frequently used within heuristic procedures. Besides the figurative and formal similarities of packing problems compared to the COSYC problem, we can state three major differences:

(1) A major task of the COSYC problem will be to *design* the "containers" or harnesses with respect to their option content, rather than just to *assign* a pre-defined set of harnesses to a car fleet.

(2) The COSYC problem, although dealing with p discrete dimensions (options), is not concerned with spatial patterns. Once a car type is assigned to a harness, the "packing pattern" is unique.

(3) As we will see, the COSYC cost function does not only depend on the containers/harnesses, but also on the objects/car types and is not very "well-behaved" in general.

2.2.2 Set Covering/Partitioning Problems

Two problems which are both theoretically and practically of crucial importance, are the set partitioning (SPP) and the set covering problem (SCP). Almost every discrete optimization problem can be tracked to the SCP, and it is well known in the field of graph theory. In practice, many scheduling problems can be stated as SCPs. Crew scheduling problems have been studied continually for many years, particularly in the airline industry (Hoffmann and Padberg, 1993). The current optimization systems of United Airlines Inc. (Graves et al., 1993) and American Airlines (Gershkoff, 1989) yield estimated annual savings of more than $15 million relative to previous enumeration techniques. Other recent applications in transportation industry can be found in vehicle crew scheduling (Ferland and Taillefer, 1992) or ocean transportation scheduling of oil companies (Brown et al., 1987). Shift or manpower scheduling problems in service organizations as hospitals, telephone companies and so forth (Vohra, 1988; Thompson, 1990; Bechtold and Jacobs, 1991), are frequently treated as SCPs.

In manufacturing, SPPs or SCPs (or variations) can be encountered for the discrete lot sizing and scheduling problem (Cattrysse et al., 1993). The task is to determine the sequence and size of production batches on one multiple-item machine which minimize cost such that dynamic demand is fulfilled without backlogging. Another application is to find a concept for automated guided vehicles (AGV) which serve a set of workstations (Bozer and Srinivasan, 1992) in a way to evenly distribute the workload among all the AGVs in the system.

Another typical example for a SCP is the location planning problem. Assume, for instance, a county has to plan for fire stations which serve its cities. The county wants to build the minimum number of fire stations needed to ensure that each city has at least one fire station within a certain driving distance (see Winston, 1994, for instance).

The SCP can be posed as a zero-one integer programming problem:

Objective

$$\min \sum_{i=1}^{m} c_i \cdot x_i \quad , \tag{2.7}$$

subject to

$$\sum_{i=1}^{m} a_{ij} \cdot x_i \geq 1 \quad j = 1, \ldots, n \quad , \tag{2.8}$$

$$x_i \in \{0, 1\} \quad i = 1, \ldots, m \quad , \tag{2.9}$$

where

m =   number of possible facility locations.

i = $1, \ldots, m$.

n =   number of customers.

j = $1, \ldots, n$.

c_i =   cost to open facility i.

$$x_i \quad = \quad \begin{cases} 1 & \text{if facility } i \text{ is opened} \\ 0 & \text{otherwise} \end{cases}$$

$$a_{ij} \quad = \quad \begin{cases} 1 & \text{if facility } i \text{ can serve customer } j \\ 0 & \text{otherwise} \end{cases}$$

The SPP can be formulated as follows:

Objective

$$\min \sum_{i=1}^{m} c_i \cdot x_i \quad , \tag{2.10}$$

subject to

$$\sum_{i=1}^{m} a_{ij} \cdot x_i = 1 \quad j = 1, \ldots, n \quad , \tag{2.11}$$

$$x_i \in \{0, 1\} \quad i = 1, \ldots, m \quad , \tag{2.12}$$

and represents the cost minimizing selection, such that each customer is served by exactly one facility.

The SPP is known to be NP-complete, the tasks of finding a feasible solution or an optimal solution have the same level of difficulty (Garey and Johnson, 1985). Most solution algorithms use relaxation techniques to obtain bounds for tree searches (Balas and Ho, 1980; Fisher and Kedia, 1990; El-Darzi and Mitra, 1992), special purpose heuristics or column generation techniques to solve the SPPs or SCPs. Due to the specific character of many applications, a lot of heuristics have been developed which exploit the special structure of the problem. Until today, there is as yet no commonly accepted best solution method with respect to computation time and quality of solutions.

2.2.3 Facility Location Problems

The general idea of the facility location problem (FLP) is to determine the cost optimal place of new facilities among a number of possible sites with the task to satisfy demand which occurs at fixed customer locations. In many cases, the number of new facilities is a priori limited by p which is a characteristic of the more general p-median location problem (PFLP). The FLP is called uncapacitated, if the facilities are of unrestricted capacity. The variety of real-life FLPs includes:

(1) Locating a new fire-department in a community.

(2) Determine the best location of a welding robot in a body shop.

(3) The most suitable place for a storage warehouse, where the company already disposes of a network of production and distribution facilities.

(4) Find the best place for a power plant to serve a geographic region.

Most FLPs can be considered as planar FLPs (Francis et al., 1983), where one assumes, that a plane represents an adequate approximation of the problem space. Facility i either shrinks to one point of $\mathbf{R}^2$ with coordinates (a_i, b_i) with a discretely assigned weight w_i, or can be thought of as a general subset $S_i \subset \mathbf{R}^2$ with a weight distribution function $w_i : S_i \rightarrow \mathbf{R}$. An application of the latter idea is a planar, rectangular shape with a uniformly distributed constant weight. Clearly, any constraints for the feasible location area may apply, where the "extreme" case is a discrete location problem. The resulting model, with a finite number of possible location scenarios can be considered as an assignment problem (Francis and White; 1974).

The cost structure is comprised of a fixed charge for opening a facility and a constant amount for supplying one unit from a particular facility to a particular customer. These volume dependent costs usually consist of product and transportation costs. If product costs are not relevant or constant for each customer, volume dependent costs are frequently a function of distance measures, such as Euclidean distance or a taxi (criss-cross) metric.

The PFLP is stated as a mixed linear integer program:

Objective

$$\min \sum_{i=1}^{m} \sum_{j=1}^{n} x_{ij} \cdot c_{ij} + \sum_{i=1}^{m} y_i \cdot f_i \quad , \tag{2.13}$$

subject to

$$\sum_{i=1}^{m} x_{ij} = d_j \quad j = 1, \ldots, n \quad , \tag{2.14}$$

$$\sum_{j=1}^{n} x_{ij} \le B \cdot y_i \quad i = 1, \ldots, m \quad , \tag{2.15}$$

$$\sum_{i=1}^{m} y_i \le p \quad , \tag{2.16}$$

$$y_j \in \{0, 1\}, \; x_{ij} \ge 0 \quad i = 1, \ldots, m, \, j = 1, \ldots, n \quad . \tag{2.17}$$

The following notation is used:

Problem parameters

m = number of possible facility locations.

p = maximum number of open facilities.

i = $1, \ldots, m$.

n = number of customers.

j = $1, \ldots, n$.

d_j = demand from customer j.

c_{ij} = cost to service customer j by facility i.

f_i = fix costs for opening facility i .

Solution variables

$$x_{ij} \quad = \quad \text{number of customers } j \text{ serviced by facility } i.$$

$$y_i \quad = \quad \begin{cases} 1 & \text{if facility } i \text{ is opened} \\ 0 & \text{otherwise} \end{cases}.$$

The objective function (2.13) seeks to minimize total costs, comprised of fixed facility opening costs and variable transportation costs. Constraint (2.14) ensures that each facility services its customers exactly according to their demand. The condition that only open facilities are productive is stated in constraint (2.15), and constraint (2.16) limits the number of open facilities to p. As one sees, no capacity constraints on any facility are stated.

PFLPs are particularly difficult to solve, if a large number of zero-one variables y_j is present. Traditional solution approaches are often based on branch-and-bound formulations, as in Efroymson and Ray (1966) or Khumawala (1972) which can still be found today in many software optimization packages. Schrage (1975) has reported a natural integer solution to the LP relaxation approach, where (2.17) is replaced by

$$y_j \geq 0, \; x_{ij} \geq 0 \quad i = 1, \ldots, m, \; j = 1, \ldots, n \quad , \tag{2.18}$$

using a variable upper bound LP programming code. Erlenkotter (1978) presented a very robust and efficient dual-based method for the FLP, where the dual formulation gets quite complicated, if a p-median constraint is present. In section 2.5, we show that the COSYC problem can be formulated as an uncapacitated p-median facility location problem.

In the following section, we will comprehensively describe the cost structure which will be utilized for the cost minimization model.

2.3   Cost Structure

In order to ensure proper power supply for all electrical options in a car, most
manufacturers use wiring harnesses where a unique wire of the bundle is assigned
to each power consuming equipment feature. Technically advanced bus structures
where only two curcuits are necessary (one to activate each option and one to supply
power), as to be found in the Lexus, for instance, have not yet entered into competition with the conventional wiring harnesses, mainly for cost and serviceability
reasons.

As most complex car modules, wiring harnesses for the engine, instrument panel,
car body and doors are almost exclusively outsourced by car manufacturers. With
Nokia, Packard Electric or the German GM subsidiary Reinshagen exist a lot of
firms that specialized in the field of harness engineering, assembly, quality control
and just-in-time delivery.

In our model cost structure, we distinguish between the following cost drivers. Costs
are assumed either to be option driven (e.g. direct material costs), or to depend on
the production volume (e.g. assembly labor), or to be caused by a particular part
number (e.g. release costs), or to depend on the option content of the car, in which
a harness is installed (e.g. warranty costs). We shall disregard all other costs and
consider them fixed. Our goal in this section is to rigorously track all costs and
eventually obtain an option based cost structure which will enable us to compute
volume and variant-dependent costs for each potential harness design during the
optimization. To this end, we will study the various cost impacts along the entire
supply chain. Figure 2.2 summarizes the qualitative result. In what follows, we will
discuss cost factors in more detail.

2.3.1   Engineering

After a new car's option specifications have been determined in the development
process, the electrical engineers start to design one wire for each electrical option

Figure 2.2: Wiring Harness Cost Drivers

	option	part number	prod. volume	car types
Engineering		YES		
Purchasing	YES		YES	
Manufacturing	YES		YES	
Logistics	YES	YES	YES	
Assembly	YES	YES	YES	YES
Aftersales	YES		YES	
Recycling	YES		YES	

h or sensor and a power are for this task which takes care of the electrical requirements as well as checks the feasibility of the wire routing topology. Only very few car companies still stick to traditional design boards in wire harness design. For many options, the design task is not performed from scratch, as their electrical realization can be partly carried over from the predecessor model. Next, the engineers have to decide upon the design of the wiring harnesses, i.e., in which way to bundle individual wires. Not very surprisingly, we recommend a procedure as COSYC to do this cost efficiently. Its effort in terms of time and hardware memory only depends on the number of considered options which is later on roughly equivalent to the number of harnesses. In the subsequent validation and release process, all costs can be assigned to particular options or part numbers. All emerging engineering labor costs can be equally split among all harness types and thus be considered variant-dependent. The depreciation allowance for soft- and hardware as well as running data base administration costs only have minor cost impact and may be divided between the harness part numbers similarly.

2.3.2   Purchasing

Cables of wiring harnesses mainly consist of copper wires, covered with plastic isolation material. At one end of each cable, there are a certain number of connectors
which are later fixed to the diverse power consumers while the other end usually runs
into a central control unit. To prevent quality problems caused by tensile or friction
forces, some harnesses (as the engine compartment harness) are protected by flexible
plastic tubes or similar materials. This additional cover can mostly be omitted for
the floor harness, where the cables don't need to bear larger displacements during
the ride. Cables are spliced either using splice boxes, or enforcing and protecting
the bifurcation with isolation tape. The number of splices is hardly dependent on
the option content. The same holds true for the number of plastic clips which are
used in the latter assembly process to fix the harness in the car body. Usually, these
clips are pre-installed in the wiring harness. After all harness part numbers are
released, the harness design is submitted to the supplier who subsequently launches
a sourcing process for the connectors, tubes, electric control units (ECUs), and so
forth. The cost of the copper wire is mainly based on the daily copper price. Thus,
material costs of option wire k in a harness j can be determined as follows:

$$C_{kj}^{mat} \; = \; m_k^{cop} \cdot (c_{cop} + c_k^{iso}) \; + \; D_{kj} \quad , \tag{2.19}$$

where m_k^{cop} is the mass of copper used, c_{cop} the average per-mass-price of copper.
$c_k^{iso} > 0$ denotes an additional factor of isolation material, proportional to the wire
length, where the sort of isolation depends on option k. D_{kj} represents the costs of
ECUs, connectors, plugs and relays. These costs depend on option k as well as on
the entire bundle j. Several door options, for instance, as power door locks, power
mirrors, power windows, and so forth, use the same multi-connection door plug.
Hence, the setup cost for the door plug can be split between most of the door option
wires in harness j. There are many more examples of option wires in a harness
which share connectors, plugs or ECUs. However, harness costs do not necessarily
have to be sub-additive in terms of the single option wire costs. For instance, there
exist a number of electrical options which can use the same power supply wire (but

not all of them at the same time) and have a rather low joint market penetration. It may be economical then to plan for a thinner power supply wire and replace it by a thicker cable in case that an unusually power consuming option combination occurs. Since the standard power supply wire is contained in the harness anyway and thus is independent of the option wires, certain option combinations can cause super-additive costs according to the above example. The material cost for harness j can be approximated as follows:

$$C_j^{mat} = \sum_{k=1}^{p} C_{kj}^{mat} + D_j \quad , \tag{2.20}$$

where D_j are the costs of taping material and plastic clips. Clearly, aggregated direct material costs depend on the option content and the harness volume. Time and man-power effort of the sourcing and procurement process are mainly depending on the option content of each harness type, rather than on its volume and hence are variant-dependent.

2.3.3 Manufacturing

In the harness manufacturing process, the option wires are provided with the required connectors, plugs and ECUs, covered in flexible plastic tubes and bundled up. The labor content is roughly proportional to the option content of each harness type and the harness volume. Packard Electric, for instance, uses a point system that measures the labor time to assemble a particular harness type. One hundred points correspond to one hour of labor; an average time for assembling an instrument panel harness is about two hours. Later on, the manufacturing time effort for each harness type is multiplied with weights, according to the regional salary levels. For Packard Electric's production plant in Chihuahua (Mexico) or Reinshagen's location in Northern Tunisia, these weights are substantially lower than for European-based manufacturing plants. As most harness suppliers have adopted a zero-defect policy, each harness is tested before it leaves the manufacturing plant. Hence, the effort for quality control depends on the harness volume, as well as on the particular harness content, since the testing time for harnesses of several option contents may be different.

The costs for testing devices, assembly tools or energy can be assigned to the different options and hardly depend on the number of harnesses or the option penetration rate.

2.3.4   Logistics

Many car manufacturers employ flexible on-line ordering-systems with their wiring harness suppliers, pursuing a (Q,R) ordering policy (see Nahmias, 1989). If a car body enters the paint-shop, for instance, a signal is transmitted to the harness supplier which releases an order for a certain harness type. These orders are consolidated until the car producer falls short of a certain harness safety stock s, e.g., s is one hour of production. The harness supplier then sends a truckload of harnesses to the car producers plant to bring the harness stock up to a sufficient level, e.g. six hours of production. The harnesses are packed in returnable boxes of different sizes which are marked with the corresponding harness part number.

Freight and shipping costs depend on the production volume as well as on the particular harness types, due to very different physical space requirements. Capital costs include stocking overhead (inventory, floor space) for the car producer in his plant and depend on piece costs (options), physical harness designs and penetration rates. The following simplistic ordering model helps to gauge all emerging logistic costs:

Since a car producers assembly schedule is frozen up to three weeks before production, only negligible harness safety stocks are necessary on the supplier side. We assume that we have m different harness types delivered by the supplier with a daily demand rate λ_j for each type j. For each harness type, there is an order size Q_j and a reorder point R_j. Transportation time T for harness j is assumed constant for simplicity. For a given truck capacity C, shipping and freight costs are c^s, and factory overhead for the car producer is c_j^o for harness type j per day. Furthermore, we assume that the harness stock is replenished immediately after the truck has arrived in the car producer's plant. This model results in a well-known order sawtooth pattern without backlogging and expected average logistic costs $C^{log}(Q_j, R_j)$:

$$C^{log}(Q_j, R_j) = \sum_{j=1}^{m} \lceil \frac{\lambda_j}{Q_j} \rceil \cdot c^s + (Q_j/2 + R_j - \lambda_j \cdot T) \cdot c_j^o \quad . \qquad (2.21)$$

The first part of the sum in (2.21) depicts daily ordering/transportation costs, the second captures the daily overhead resulting from average safety stock. By an optimal choice of Q_j and R_j, C^{log} can be minimized.

2.3.5 Assembly

During the assembly process, the engine harness, dashboard harness, body harness, and so forth, are installed in the car body on the assembly line. One worker periodically reads the production schedule and prepares the harnesses for in-line-sequence installation. For this reason, the harness boxes are stored close to the assembly line and placed such that material handling costs are minimized. The job content of harness installation at each work station is described by standardized work sheets which also include time durations. Hence, harness preparation and installation times both depend on the harness type. Furthermore, assembly times may also depend on the option content of the car which does not necessarily have to coincide with the harness option content. For instance, loose cables with large and heavy connectors, as for cruise control, cause acoustic quality problems due to clattering against structural parts or can even damage smaller connectors and cause short circuits. If a car does not contain the cruise control option, the assigned harness however does, the critical plug has to be isolated with foam rubber and firmly tied to the cable. Vice versa, some wires may have been already taped by the supplier and have to be loosened at the line, if the corresponding car type requires the connection. Whether a wire is already taped by the supplier mainly depends on penetration of the particular options, hence labor costs, and line balancing issues. Hence, costs of installing the same harness in different cars may differ. Furthermore, scheduling and control labor effort additionally depends on the harness part numbers.

2.3.6   Aftersales and Recycling

Aftersales costs are mainly restricted to warranty costs due to functional failure of a harness. These are determined by the number of defects, hence the production volume, but also on the cost of the defect option wire itself. At the end of a car's life cycle, it can be returned to the car company, that recycles or even reuses predominantly plastic parts. A wiring harness can be almost completely recycled, where plastic parts and the copper wire are melted down. Recycling costs clearly depend on the produced car volume and the particular option wires.

2.3.7   Example

To illustrate how costs are assigned during the optimization, we consider the following four engine harness types, where an "x" indicates the option dependency of a harness:

Harness Type	1.6 ltr.	1.8 ltr.	ABS	Cruise	costs ($)
1	x				44.00
2	x		x	x	69.00
3		x		x	55.00
4		x	x	x	72.00

The cost for single options (including installation) are:

1.6 ltr. engine	:	$44.00
1.8 ltr. engine	:	$47.00
ABS (Anti-Lock-Brake System)	:	$17.00
Cruise Control	:	$8.00

We furthermore assume that the cost for removing isolation tape of the cruise control option is $0.12 per car, the fix costs for each part number are assumed $10,000.

The above harnesses are assigned to the following car variants:

Car Type	1.6 ltr.	1.8 ltr.	ABS	Cruise	# cars	harness	costs ($)
1	x				70,000	1	3,080,000
2	x		x		1,000	2	69,000
3	x		x	x	5,000	2	345,600
4		x			20,000	3	1,100,000
5		x	x		40,000	4	2,880,000
6		x		x	25,000	3	1,378,000
7		x	x	x	8,000	4	576,960
						Σ_{vol}	9,429,560
						Σ_{var}	40,000
						Σ_{total}	9,469,560

Costs amount to $9,469,560, if the cheapest feasible harness is installed in each car variant. The difference between actual harness costs and the mere option costs are mainly due to the necessity to give away the cruise control cable for some vehicles.

Designing one additional harness with optimized content (1.8 ltr. engine, ABS) yields a reduction of harness costs by $305,200 or $1.81 per car.

The cost optimal harness design consists of six harnesses which exactly correspond to the car variants one and three through seven. There is no monetary justification for a seventh harness (corresponding to car variant two), because savings in volume-dependent costs exceed the additional fix costs of $ 10,000 per harness.

In the next section, we focus on the question how actual sales data can be linked with forecast data in order to obtain an appropriate data base for the optimization procedure.

2.4 Modeling Demand By Forecast Disaggregation

2.4.1 Motivation

An indispensable prerequisite for successful planning activities along the entire production process is a detailed prediction of future demand for a particular product. Anticipating demand at an early stage in a manufacturer's product development process, for instance, has a great impact on product costs, since a large fraction of these is already determined in the design phase. Later on, safety stock and thus holding costs depend on the quality of forecast demand and length of forecast horizon.

In the automobile industry, forecasts typically estimate the absolute penetration of options, as engine size, transmission, body style, electrical options, colors, etc., or of some major option combinations (e.g. engine/transmission split or engine/body split) in order to obtain stable order schemes or business plans. In general, forecasts for arbitrary option combinations or combinations of more than two options (higher order forecasts) are only available for very short time horizons (less than 4 weeks) for production planning purposes. These are exclusively based on real order data. NUMMI's production planning, for instance, uses a very rigid ordering scheme, the so-called *katashiki* which does not allow any changes in the major option content of a car (type, body style, engine, transmission, interior/exterior colors) within eight weeks before the car is actually produced. Minor options (ABS, airbags, etc.) are frozen three weeks before the car is built. Since NUMMI purchases engines and transmissions exclusively from Toyota Motor Corp., Japan which require shipping times of six to seven weeks, the *katashiki* enables NUMMI to avoid almost all safety stock of these spacious, heavy and expensive components.

Besides these short-term forecasts, it is necessary to have good demand estimations for longer periods of time, as approximately two years for the design of wiring harnesses or the general conception of a car product program. For business plans, project budgeting and strategic management decisions, forecasts even for the next ten years may be required. For these expanded time horizons, conventional marketing tools, as surveys, car clinics, or analytical methods can only be used to predict penetrations of single options or some few option combinations for reasons of complexity. These aggregated forecasts may not be sufficient for all purposes.

To design the wires, relays, plugs and terminals of a set of wiring harnesses, one needs an estimate of the demand for a particular car type, broken down to its option content. Such a desired disaggregated car pool can be represented as a file of records. Each record consists of an integer number greater than zero (predicted demand) and a binary number of q digits $0010111\ldots01$. The r-th digit tells, whether option q is contained in this car variant (value 1), or not (value 0). Theoretically, such a file can consist of 2^q records, if there is demand for each possible car type. In practice, there are logical (each car variant can only have one body style, engine, transmission, etc.) and technical restrictions which prevent some options from occurring simultaneously. Even though, the length of the file is growing exponentially with increasing q.

In the following section we show how to obtain a disaggregated car pool, using low order forecasts and current sales data. The idea is to adapt current sales data in a way that it is consistent with the marketing forecasts. We hereby emphasize the underlying assumption that demand for higher order option combinations does not significantly change within the forecast period, unless this change is quantified in the forecasts.

2.4.2 Problem Formulation

We start with a data base containing information about current car sales (e.g. the last 3-8 months) where each sold car variant is described by its option content and sales volume. This car data base does not exactly reflect demand, but also contains the customers response to a given supply or salesmen effectiveness. Therefore, its interpretation depends on the prevalence of "make-to-order" production and showroom sales. In any case, it retains its advantage of high disaggregation and option interdependencies over almost all empirical marketing research data of this type.

In addition, these car variants may not be consistent with future product information (e.g. two years later), since some options may vanish, others may be new and some option combinations may not be feasible anymore. Redundant options or option combinations can be easily deleted from each car variant of the sales file. Most "new" options just replace old options (for instance, a new 16 valve, 2.0 liter engine replaces the former 8 valve, 2.0 liter engine). The only difficult case is how to establish an entirely new, non-standard option (for instance, a new anti-theft device). One solution is to logically couple such an option to the trim levels of the car model and distribute it according to quotas (e.g., 10% for the basic level, 25% for the advanced equipment and 65% for the luxury car). This method requires a certain amount of experience and can be combined with a scenario approach: for "critical" options one can develop several distribution scenarios which lead to several disaggregated car scenarios.

Having accomplished the upper procedure, the resulting car scenario (or car scenarios) still has sales character, although the considered car variants now correspond to the new product program. The idea is to find a non-negative multiplier for the number of sales of each car variant, such that their product creates a car scenario which is consistent with the marketing forecasts for options/combinations. For this purpose, we use the following notations:

$$
\begin{aligned}
n &= \text{number of considered car variants.} \\
i &= 1, \ldots, n. \\
m &= \text{number of forecasted options/combinations.} \\
j &= 1, \ldots, m \\
k_i &= \text{number of car variants } i \text{ sold.} \\
\mathbf{k} &= (k_1, \ldots, k_n). \\
b_j &= \text{absolute forecast for option/combination } j, \ (b_j > 0). \\
\mathbf{b} &= (b_1, \ldots, b_m). \\
l_i &= \text{lower bound for decision variables } (l_i > 0). \\
x_i &= \text{decision variable, multiplier for car variant } i. \\
\mathbf{x} &= (x_1, \ldots, x_n).
\end{aligned}
$$

$$a_{ij} = \begin{cases} 1 & \text{if car } i \text{ contains option/combination } j \\ 0 & \text{otherwise} \end{cases}.$$

$$\mathbf{A} = \text{Mat}(a_{ij}).$$

Consider the following system of m linear equations:

$$\sum_{i=1}^{n} a_{ji} k_i x_i = b_j \qquad \text{for } j = 1 \dots m \quad . \tag{2.22}$$

The scalar $d_i = k_i \cdot x_i$ can now be interpreted as the demand for car type i, provided that $x_i \geq 0$. In fact, we don't want to reduce the complexity of the car variants by allowing $x_i = 0$. Thus, we want $x_i \geq l_i$, where l_i is a strictly positive lower bound for the multipliers.

Since typical values are $n = 20,000$ and $m = 100$, (2.22) has many more columns than rows. From an algebraic point of view, we know that system (2.22) has a solution, if and only if $rank(\mathbf{A}) = rank(\mathbf{A}, \mathbf{b})$. In this case, the solution space is linear and its dimension is equal to $n - m$.

Due to the multidimensionality of the solution space, we need additional constraints to obtain a unique solution for the multipliers. Requiring that the solution $\mathbf{x}$ minimizes the Euclidean distance to a given vector $\mathbf{p}$, $\|\mathbf{x} - \mathbf{p}\|_2$, leads to the so-called *Gaussian Normal Equation*

$$\mathbf{A}\mathbf{A}^{\mathbf{T}}\mathbf{t} = \mathbf{b} - \mathbf{A}\mathbf{p} \quad , \tag{2.23}$$

which is usually solved by decomposing $\mathbf{A}\mathbf{A}^{\mathbf{T}}$ and finally solving for $\mathbf{x}$

$$\mathbf{x} = \mathbf{b} + \mathbf{A}^{\mathbf{T}}\mathbf{t} \quad . \tag{2.24}$$

Unfortunately, even if the components of $\mathbf{p}$ are chosen very large, these constraints do not imply that all components of $\mathbf{x}$ are positive. In general, there do not exist such side constraints which reduce the dimension of the solution space by $n - m - 1$ and guarantee that each multiplier x_i is positive.

Instead of solving for the multipliers x_i directly, we show in the next paragraph, how to use a linear programming approach instead.

2.4.3   Optimization Approach

For an arbitrary $\bar{\mathbf{x}} = (\bar{x}_1, \ldots, \bar{x}_n)$ we define the absolute error e_j of (2.22) for $j = 1, \ldots, m$ by

$$e_j = \left| b_j - \sum_{i=1}^{n} a_{ij}\bar{x}_i \right| \quad , \tag{2.25}$$

and the relative error r_j by

$$r_j = \frac{e_j}{b_j} \quad . \tag{2.26}$$

Our goal is to minimize the relative error $\|r_j\|$ which is a nonlinear function of the multipliers x_i. Introducing two dummy variables z_j^+, z_j^-, we can state this nonlinear optimization problem as a linear optimization problem which is significantly easier to solve:

Objective

$$\min \sum_{j=1}^{m} \frac{z_j^+ + z_j^-}{b_j} \quad , \tag{2.27}$$

subject to

$$z_j^+ - z_j^- = b_j - \sum_{i=1}^{n} a_{ij}k_i x_i \qquad j = 1, \ldots, m \quad , \tag{2.28}$$

$$x_i \geq l_i \qquad i = 1, \ldots, n \quad , \tag{2.29}$$

$$z_j^+ \geq 0 \qquad j = 1, \ldots, m \quad , \tag{2.30}$$

$$z_j^- \geq 0 \qquad j = 1, \ldots, m \quad . \tag{2.31}$$

The dummy variables z_j^+ and z_j^- can be interpreted as the positive, respectively negative deviation from the forecast $b_j - \sum_{i=1}^{n} a_{ij}k_i x_i$. The linear program has m nontrivial constraints and can be solved by standard linear programming methods.

Usually, it is necessary to rescale the problem due to the large difference in magnitudes of $\mathbf{x}$ and $\mathbf{k}$ to avoid numerical difficulties. If we choose a least square method instead of minimizing the relative error, we need to apply quadratic solution methods.

Again, we emphasize the meaning of the resulting disaggregated car scenario: all initial car variants have been maintained, no new car variants have been added.

The car scenario is now consistent with all available marketing forecasts, where we assumed that demand for option combinations which are not mentioned in the forecast, does not significantly differ from the original sales figures.

Example 1: Assume, we have to disaggregate forecasts for car variants which can be described by three options. Each car variant can be thought of as a three-digit aggregation of zeros or ones, where a one at the r-th place ($1 \leq r \leq 3$) denotes, that the car contains option r, and a zero indicates the opposite. Consider the following car variant sales data.

Car	combination	sales
1	1 0 0	5,000
2	1 1 0	3,500
3	1 1 1	1,000
4	0 0 1	500

and the following forecasts for options 1,2 and 3:

option	forecast
1	11,000
2	3,000
3	3,000

Thus, we have $n = 4$ and $m = 3$, $\mathbf{k} = (5,000; 3,500; 1,000; 500)$. Furthermore, $\mathbf{b} = (11,000; 3,000; 3,000)$, and

$$
A = \begin{pmatrix} 1 & 1 & 1 & 0 \\ 0 & 1 & 1 & 0 \\ 0 & 0 & 1 & 1 \end{pmatrix} \quad . \tag{2.32}
$$

Since we may expect relative market share stability for each car variant, we define the lower bounds $(l_1, l_2, l_3, l_4) = (1., 1., 1., 1.)$. Solving the corresponding linear optimization problem with LINGO, yields

$$
\begin{aligned}
x_1 &= 1.30 \\
x_2 &= 1.00 \\
x_3 &= 1.00 \\
x_4 &= 4.00
\end{aligned}
$$

for the multipliers and an objective value of 0.5. The new forecast car scenario is of the form:

Car	combination	demand
1	1 0 0	6,500
2	1 1 0	3,500
3	1 1 1	1,000
4	0 0 1	2,000

with resulting option volumes:

option	forecast
1	11,000
2	4,500
3	3,000

As one sees, resulting options volumes coincide with the forecasts for options 1 and 3. The volume of option 2 has been overestimated by 50%, because its historic volume has been 4,500 units already, and we haven't allowed a volume reduction of any car type by letting $\lambda = (1., 1., 1., 1.)$.

In general, the presented method combines the knowledge of current option interdependencies and future demand. Hence, the resulting disaggregated car data will be a good and detailed predictor of future sales, provided that option correlations are reasonably stable over time and option forecasts are accurate.

In the following sections we will see, how disaggregated forecast car data are used for the stochastic optimization of customized wiring harnesses.

2.5 Stochastic Model Formulation

In this section we will formulate the general COSYC problem as a p-median facility location problem. The central task will be to find the cost optimal harness designs and determine their number in order to assign them to certain car types. Since harness production capacity is assumed to be unlimited, we will restrict our considerations to the less general, uncapacitated case. Due to the potential uncertainty of the underlying car data, we consider several car "scenarios" with assigned probabilities.

2.5.1 Model Notations and Definitions

As a reference, all variables needed for the model definition, problem formulation and the algorithmic part are stated below:

Option related variables

q = the number of harness relevant options.

r = $1, \ldots, q$.

$\mathcal{B}$ = $\{0, 1\}$.

Car related variables

s^* = number of considered demand scenarios.

s $=$ $1, \ldots, s^{*}$.

n_s $=$ the quantity of car variants in demand scenario s.

i $=$ $1, \ldots, n$.

π_s $=$ probability for demand scenario s.

d_{is} $=$ demand for car variant i, demand scenario s.

Harness related variables

m $=$ the number of possible harness types available.

j $=$ $1, \ldots, m$.

p $=$ the maximum number of harness types (physical span).

a_{ij} $=$ $\begin{cases} 1 & \text{if harness } j \text{ is feasible for car type } i \\ 0 & \text{otherwise} \end{cases}$

Harness Costs

c_{ij} $=$ costs to equip a car type i with harness j.

f_j $=$ fix variant-dependent costs of harness type j.

Solution Variables

y_j $=$ $\begin{cases} 1 & \text{if harness } j \text{ is produced} \\ 0 & \text{otherwise} \end{cases}$

x_{ijs} $=$ number of car types i, scenario s, equipped with harness j.

As mentioned above, the database for the optimization consists of car fleets, characterized by their option content and demand (see section 2.4). With the above notation, each car type i can be uniquely expressed as a q-digit Boolean vector $\{v_1, \ldots, v_q\} \in \mathcal{B}^q$, with $v_r = 1$, if the car variant requires option r, $v_r = 0$, otherwise, for all $r \leq q$.

A **demand scenario** s consists of car variants $1, \ldots, n_s$, where to each car variant i_s is assigned corresponding demand d_{is}. To each of the s^{*} demand scenarios considered, we assign probabilities π_s, where

$$\sum_{s=1}^{s^*} \pi_s = 1 \quad .$$
(2.33)

In analogy, a **harness set** of order m consists of m harnesses. Each harness j can equivalently be expressed as a q-digit Boolean vector $\{h_1, \ldots, h_q\} \in \mathcal{B}^q$, with $h_r = 1$, if option r is contained in the harness, $h_r = 0$, otherwise, for all $r \leq q$.

A harness j ($\{h_1, \ldots, h_q\}$) will be called **feasible** for a car type i ($\{v_1, \ldots, v_q\}$), if

$$1 \geq h_k \geq v_r \geq 0 \quad r = 1, \ldots, q \quad .$$
(2.34)

A harness set will be called **feasible** for demand scenario s, if it contains at least one feasible harness for each car type is. The design and thus feasibility of an optimal harness set strongly depends on the forecasts for future cars option requirements. Surely, there may arise demand for car variants, for which no feasible harness exists. To assure feasibility in this case, the car manufacturer needs to plan for so-called **mandatory harnesses**. In the simplest case, one "super-harness" (1111..11) would suffice to guarantee feasibility of a harness set. However, there exist option wires (e.g. for airbags) which can not be taped, if they remain unconnected. For some plugs, taping may not be sufficient to avoid quality problems (noise, short circuits), other wires can not be "shut down" that way because they are meant to transmit continuous signals. Hence, r mandatory options cause 2^r mandatory harnesses.

Example 2: Assume, six options have to be satisfied by a harness set, where options one and two are mandatory options. The resulting four mandatory harnesses are:

Harness Type	Option Content
1	0 0 1 1 1 1
2	1 0 1 1 1 1
3	0 1 1 1 1 1
4	1 1 1 1 1 1

The simplest way to take mandatory harnesses into account is to interpret them as additional car types and add them to all car scenarios with a minimum penetration of 1, for instance.

To express the infeasibility of harness j for a car type i, we will set c_{ij} equal to a very large number. Otherwise, c_{ij} will be the cost to equip all d_{is} cars of type i, scenario s, with harness j. We are now ready to formulate the COSYC problem.

2.5.2   Model Formulation

The COSYC problem can be stated in the following way:

Objective function

$$\min \ \sum_{s=1}^{s^*} \pi_s \left[\sum_{j=1}^{m} \sum_{i=1}^{n} c_{ij} \cdot x_{ijs} \right] + \sum_{j=1}^{m} y_j \cdot f_j \ , \tag{2.35}$$

subject to

$$\sum_{j=1}^{m} x_{ijs} = d_{is} \quad i = 1, \dots, n_s, \ s = 1, \dots, s^* \ , \tag{2.36}$$

$$\sum_{s=1}^{s^*} \sum_{i=1}^{n_s} x_{ijs} \leq B \cdot y_j \quad j = 1, \dots, m \ , \tag{2.37}$$

$$\sum_{j=1}^{m} y_j \leq p \ , \tag{2.38}$$

$$x_{ijs} \geq 0 \quad i = 1, \dots, n_s, \ j = 1, \dots, m, \ s = 1, \dots, s^* \ , \tag{2.39}$$

$$y_j \in \{0, 1\}, \quad j = 1, \dots, m \ . \tag{2.40}$$

Constraint (2.36) assures, that exactly one harness type will be assigned to each car type. According to constraint (2.37), a harness type can only be assigned to a car type, if the harness is actually produced. The p-median constraint (2.38) limits the number of different harness types due to the physical factory span.

The COSYC problem is a mixed integer program and has many constraints Typical values from practical problems are $n = 20,000$, $p = 50$, where m, the number of potential candidate harness designs, equals $2^q - 1$. Although, we can a priori eliminate a certain percentage of inappropriate harness candidates, we can not reduce the problem size substantially. The large number of car types does not allow for a effective pre-screening of harnesses. Hence, the number of constraints of the COSYC problem grows exponentially with the number of options considered. Moreover, integer programming problems are known to be hard to solve even with few constraints (see Garey and Johnson (1979), for instance).

The following example shows that a harness which belongs to an optimal harness design for a fixed value p, does not necessarily have to be optimal, if the physical factory span p is increased.

Example 3: Consider the following four-option demand scenario ($s^* = 1$):

$$\{(1100; 50,000), (1010; 40,000), (0111; 5,000)\} \quad , \qquad (2.41)$$

which means, that 50,000 cars with option combination one and two, 40,000 cars with options one and three and 5,000 cars with combination two to four are produced. Let the costs of options one and four be \$8, for options two and three \$3, respectively.

Without mandatory options, the only mandatory harness is 1111, with costs of \$2,090,000 (overall volume × cost of 1111 (\$22)). For m=2, the cost optimal harness set consists of the mandatory harness and an additional harness 1110, with the following volumes produced (without fix costs):

Car Type	Harness Type	quantity	costs (\$)
1 1 0 0	1 1 1 0	50,000	700,000
1 0 1 0	1 1 1 0	40,000	560,000
0 1 1 1	1 1 1 1	5,000	110,000
		Σ	1,370,000

Options two and three are relatively inexpensive compared to one and four. Designing one harness for both high-volume car variants and to give away the low cost options causes less costs, than to design a corresponding harness for car variant one

(1100). Consequently, car variant two then requires the mandatory harness (1111) and one loses 40,000 times the value for option four.

Considering the case $m = 3$, there is no more justification for harness 1110, because with two harnesses 1100 and 1010 we can exactly cover the option requests of the two high-volume car variants and only loose 5,000 times option one, by assigning the mandatory harness to car variant three:

Car Type	Harness Type	quantity	costs (\$)
1 1 0 0	1 1 0 0	50,000	550,000
1 0 1 0	1 0 1 0	40,000	440,000
0 1 1 1	1 1 1 1	5,000	110,000
		Σ	1,100,000

This demonstrates that a harness, contained in the cost optimal set of order m, does not need to occur in a optimal higher order set.

To be able to evaluate a heuristic method over all instances a priori, we will introduce a *performance measure* (compare Nemhauser and Wolsey, 1988). One way to obtain a meaningful evaluation is by performing a worst-case analysis. We call $\mathcal{I}$ the set of instances of initial demand/cost scenarios. Let $z_C(I)$ denote the optimal solution of the COSYC problem (2.35) subject to constraints (2.36)-(2.40). Suppose we have found a heuristic algorithm H which finds a feasible solution $z_H(I)$ for each instance $I \in \mathcal{I}$. Since we want our performance measure to be independent of the scaling of the objective function, we will choose an relative error measure. We say that heuristic H has *worst-case performance* P_H, if

$$P_H = \sup\{P \,|\, z_C(I) \geq P_H \cdot z_H(I) \quad \forall I \in \mathcal{I}\} \quad . \tag{2.42}$$

From definition, we have $P_H \in [0; 1]$, and H guarantees to find a solution of value at most $(100/P_H)\%$ of the minimum value for all instances $I \in \mathcal{I}$.

By relating the p-median facility minimization problem to a k-clique node covering problem from graph theory one obtains the following classic result:

Lemma 4: *The p-median facility minimization problem with performance measure $P_H \geq P$ is NP-hard for every $P > 0$.*

This shows that (in contrary to the p-median facility maximization problem) there is no "reliably good" efficient heuristic for the COSYC problem, unless P=NP.

For moderate problem sizes however, commercial software, such as LINGO, can be used to solve the COSYC problem straightforward. The following example expands the data from the Example in section 2.4 and illustrates the key steps.

Example 5: Assume, one has to design optimal harnesses for a three-option module, as for instance the driver's door, consisting of electric power door lock (option 1), power window (option 2) and power mirror (option 3). According to forecasts, there will be a demand for four major option combinations/car variants (again, $s^* = 1$):

Car Type	Option Content	Demand
1	1 0 0	5,000
2	1 1 0	3,500
3	1 1 1	1,000
4	0 0 1	500

The set of all possible candidate harnesses for the above demand scenario, including corresponding material costs is:

Harness Type	Option Content	Cost ($)
1	1 0 0	1
2	0 1 0	1
3	0 0 1	1
4	1 1 0	2
5	0 1 1	2
6	1 0 1	2
7	1 1 1	3

We want to find the cost optimal subset of the presented seven harnesses, such that each car variant finds a feasible harness in this subset. For each harness type which we include in the optimal subset, we have to bear a fix cost of $100. We define the following cost matrix C, where c_{ij} denote material plus labor costs to install harness j in car i. The large number $c_{ij} = M$ indicates that harness j is infeasible for car type i:

$$
C = \begin{pmatrix}
2 & M & M & 3 & M & 3 & 4 \\
M & M & M & 4 & M & M & 5 \\
M & M & M & M & M & M & 6 \\
M & M & 2 & M & 3 & 3 & 4
\end{pmatrix} .
$$

We can now formulate the problem as follows:

Objective function

$$
\min \quad \sum_{j=1}^{7} \sum_{i=1}^{4} c_{ij} \cdot x_{ij} + \sum_{j=1}^{7} y_j \cdot f_j \tag{2.43}
$$

subject to

$$
\sum_{j=1}^{7} x_{ij} = d_i \quad i = 1, \ldots, 4 \quad , \tag{2.44}
$$

$$
\sum_{i=1}^{4} x_{ij} \leq B \cdot y_j \quad j = 1, \ldots, 7 \quad , \tag{2.45}
$$

$$
\sum_{j=1}^{T} y_j \leq p \quad , \tag{2.46}
$$

$$
x_{ij} \geq 0 \quad i = 1, \ldots, 4, \; j = 1, \ldots, 7 \quad , \tag{2.47}
$$

$$
y_j \in \{0, 1\} \quad j = 1, \ldots, 4 \quad . \tag{2.48}
$$

This mixed integer program was solved with LINGO with the following result:

p	Cost	Harnesses for Cars 1..4
1	45,600	7 7 7 7
2	35,700	1 7 7 7
3	32,300	1 4 7 7
4	31,400	1 4 7 3

However, with this approach we will not be able to solve a problem with a large quantity q of options, because the number of candidate harnesses is exponentially increasing with q. Thus, it will not be possible to store and process all available harnesses. There is a need for methods that do not consider "unreasonable" harness candidates, such as no.2 in the example. In the next section, we present and analyze potential solution methods.

In the next section, we will introduce several potential solution methods and perform a tractability analysis of the COSYC problem.

2.6 Solution Methods and Model Analysis

In this section, we present three algorithmic approaches to solve the COSYC problem. The first method employs relaxation techniques to obtain lower bounds for a subsequent branch-and-bound phase, while the second is based on column generation. The third method is a greedy heuristic which takes advantage of the special structure of the problem or can be combined with a simulated annealing procedure.

Tractable solution algorithms for the large-scale COSYC problem are difficult to find, because we can not consider all potential candidate harnesses simultaneously. Moreover, we have shown in section 2.3 that the costs of one option wire can depend on the entire option design of the harness. Consequently, volume dependent costs are neither sub- nor super-additive in general, and we can not expect to find globally optimal solutions from a solution method with polynomial run-time. Nevertheless, "good" sub-optimal solutions may be acceptable for two main reasons:

1. If we are using several forecast car scenarios, assigned probabilities will not add up to one in the real world. Not all possible car scenarios can be considered, and hence a computationally, globally optimal solution of the model will always turn out to be sub-optimal in the real world. Therefore, it makes only little sense to try to achieve an exactness in the solution procedures that is more restrictive than the error in the initial data.

2. The conception of wiring harnesses for a car line is not a static decision. Once the harnesses are released, they will surely be changed several times during the life cycle of the vehicle due the shortened forecast horizon, changes in the supplier's pricing policy, major running model changes, and so forth. Changing the harnesses means in practice mostly to increase their number or to enhance their design by additional option wires. Very seldom, the number of harness types is reduced. To hedge against these potential changes, it is sensible to consciously choose a smaller quantity of harnesses than an optimal solution would recommend. A slightly smaller number will imply increased costs but still leaves one on the downward slope of the cost function. Thus, a moderate addition of harnesses results in only incremental cost increases.

2.6.1   Branch-and-Bound and Relaxation

The method we present in this section is based on an enumerative approach. Most commercial codes use a similar algorithm to solve mixed-integer programs. We generally distinguish between two enumeration approaches for combinatorial optimization problems. *Total enumeration* successively generates each feasible integer solution $y = (y_1, \ldots, y_m) \in Y$, where Y is the set of extreme points of a bounded polytope. For each fixed vector y, we solve the corresponding linear program COSYC(y). If the optimal solution $z(y)$ is smaller than the "best" current feasible solution, they are interchanged. We continue in this fashion until all feasible integer solutions y are processed. Eventually, we have found the global minimum of COSYC, z_C. This "brute-force" approach is only tractable problems of moderate size. For $m = 15$ and one processed y-value per second, total enumeration needs more than 9 hours to solve the problem. *Implicit enumeration* tries to successively exclude subsets of Y, which do not contain the optimal solution. The wide-spread branch-and-bound method follows the divide-and-conquer principle: if it is too difficult to solve the original problem, it may be easier to divide the problem in smaller subproblems, solve them, and put the results together. Implicit enumeration is only tractable if we do not have to divide Y in too many subsets. In the worst case, implicit enumeration is as time consuming as total enumeration.

Let $\{Y_k \mid k = 1, \ldots, K\}$ be a partition of Y, i.e. $\bigcup_{k=1}^{K} Y_k = S$ and $Y_k \cap Y_{k'} = \emptyset$ for $k, k' = 1, \ldots, K$, $k \neq k'$. For each Y_k, let COSYC(k) denote the corresponding COSYC problem, where all solution vectors y are drawn from Y_k. Let z_k be the optimal solution of the COSYC problem, if we limit the integer vector y to the set Y_k. Then,

$$z_C = \max\{z(Y_k) \mid k = 1, \ldots, K\} \quad . \tag{2.49}$$

We can consequently remove a set Y_k from our scheme, if any one of the following three alternatives holds:

1. $Y_k = \emptyset$ (infeasiblity)

2. z_k is known (optimality)

3. $z_k \geq z_C$ (value dominance)

We will now state a general branch-and-bound algorithm for solving the formal COSYC problem $\min\{F(Y)\}$. For this purpose, let $\mathcal{T}$ denote a collection of problems $\{MIP_k\}$, with corresponding feasible sets Y_k ($Y_k \subseteq Y$), and optimal solutions $z_k = F(Y_k)$. Assume that for each problem in $\mathcal{T}$, we know a lower bound $\underline{z}^k \leq z_k$.

BRANCH-AND-BOUND

Step 1 (Initialize):
$\mathcal{T} =$ COSYC, $Y^* = Y$, $\underline{z}^0 = -\infty$, $z_* = \infty$.

Step 2 (Terminate):
If $\mathcal{T} = \emptyset$, then the solution $y^* \in Y$ with $z_* = F(y^*)$ is optimal.

Step 3 (Select and Find Lower Bound):

Select a problem COSYC(k) from $\mathcal{T}$ and let $\mathcal{T} = \mathcal{T}-$COSYC(k). Find a lower bound z_k for COSYC(k) and let y_k be an optimal solution (if it exists!).

Step 4 (Removing):

1. If $z_k \geq z_*$, then go to Step 2.

2. Else, if $y_k \notin Y_k$, then go to Step 5.

3. Else, if $y_k \in Y_k$ and $F(y_k) < z_*$, then let $z_* = F(y_k)$. Delete all problems with $z^k \geq z_*$ from T. If $F(y_k) = z_k$, then go to Step 2; otherwise go to Step 5.

Step 5 (Divide):

Let $\{Y_{kk'}\}_{k'=1}^K$ be a division of Y_k. Let $\mathcal{T} = \mathcal{T}+$COSYC(kk')$_{k'=1}^K$, where $z^{kk'} = z_k$ for $k' = 1, \ldots, K$. Go to Step 2.

Relaxation

We still need to know strategies how to obtain lower bounds z_k for our subproblems min $F(Y_k)$. Since we do not want to solve another MIP for obtaining bounds, this is usually done by solving an appropriate relaxation of the original problem. We will present two ways for doing so, strong LP relaxation and Lagrangian relaxation. In strong LP relaxation, constraint (2.40) of the COSYC problem is lessened to

$$y_j \in [0;1] \quad \forall j \leq m \quad . \tag{2.50}$$

Let $\underline{z}$ be the minimum cost of the strong LP relaxation. Then we have

$$\underline{z} \leq z_C \quad , \tag{2.51}$$

i.e. the optimal LP relaxation solution is never worse than the optimal solution of the original problem. Let LP_k be the strong LP relaxation of COSYC(k), and let $\underline{z}_k$ denote the value of an optimal solution of LP_k. We can remove a set Y_k from our scheme, if any one of the following three alternatives holds:

1. LP_k is infeasible

2. An optimal solution $\underline{y}_k$ of LP_k is a feasible solution of COSYC(k)

3. $\underline{z}_k \geq z_*$, where z_* is the value of a feasible solution of COSYC.

Condition 1 implies $Y_k = \emptyset$. Condition 2 implies that $\underline{y}_k$ is

$$\underline{z} \leq z_C \quad , \tag{2.52}$$

an optimal solution of COSYC(k), and condition 3 implies that $\underline{z}_k \geq z_C$. However, we must finish the optimization of LP_k before we can remove a problem IP_k from our scheme due to value dominance.

To utilize a Lagrangian relaxation method, let $\lambda = (\lambda_{11}, \ldots, \lambda_{n_s \cdot s^*})$ be real valued multipliers of constraint (2.36) of the original COSYC problem. The Lagrangian function L_C is then defined as

$$
\begin{aligned}
L_C(x, y, \lambda) &= \sum_{s=1}^{s^*} \pi_s \sum_{j=1}^{m} \sum_{i=1}^{n_s} c_{ij} \cdot x_{ijs} + \sum_{j=1}^{m} f_j \cdot y_j - \sum_{s=1}^{s^*} \sum_{i=1}^{n_s} \lambda_{is} \left(\sum_{j=1}^{m} x_{ijs} - d_{is} \right) \\
&= \sum_{j=1}^{m} \left(\sum_{s=1}^{s^*} \sum_{i=1}^{n_s} (c_{ij} - \lambda_{is}) \cdot x_{ijs} + f_j \cdot y_j \right) + \sum_{s=1}^{s^*} \sum_{i=1}^{n_s} \lambda_{is} \cdot d_{is} \quad . \tag{2.53}
\end{aligned}
$$

The Lagrangian problem (LAG_C) of COSYC can be stated as follows.

Objective

$$z_{LAG}(\lambda) = \min_{x,y} L_C(x, y, \lambda) \quad , \tag{2.54}$$

subject to

$$0 \leq x_{ijs} \leq y_j \leq 1 \quad i = 1, \ldots, n_s, \; j = 1, \ldots, m \; s = 1, \ldots, s^* \quad , \tag{2.55}$$

$$\sum_{j=1}^{m} y_j \leq p \quad , \tag{2.56}$$

$$y_j \in \{0, 1\}, \quad x_{ijs} \geq 0 \quad i = 1, \ldots, n_s, \; j = 1, \ldots, m, \; s = 1, \ldots, s^* \quad , \tag{2.57}$$

where we have chosen a slightly less compact formulation of the problem replacing (2.37) by (2.55). In the Lagrangian problem, we have shifted the equality constraint on the x_{ijs} variables to the objective function and equipped it with a penalty

λ_{is} which increases the objective, if the constraint is violated. The corresponding Lagrangian dual (LD_k) is given by

Objective

$$z_{LD} = \max_{\lambda} z_{LAG}(\lambda) \quad , \tag{2.58}$$

subject to

$$\lambda_{is} \geq 0 \quad i = 1, \ldots, n_s, \ s = 1, \ldots, s^* \quad . \tag{2.59}$$

From weak duality we know that $z_{LD} \leq z_C$. The coefficient matrix of constraints (2.55) and (2.56) with regard to the y_j variables is

$$
\begin{pmatrix}
 & I^m & & & \\
 & I^m & & & \\
 & \vdots & & \vdots & \\
 & I^m & & & \\
1 & 1 & \cdots & 1 & 1
\end{pmatrix}
\tag{2.60}
$$

consisting of $\sum_{s=1}^{s^*} n_s$ unit matrices of size m, and is hence *totally unimodular*, i.e. each square submatrix has determinant 1 or -1. The reason is that the transposed is an interval matrix (consecutive ones in rows) and is therefore known to be totally unimodular. A classical result of Geoffrion (1974) shows that $z_{LD} = z$, i.e., the optimal value of the Lagrangian relaxation equals the optimal solution of the strong LP relaxation.

The Lagrangian problem (LAG_C) can be solved analytically for fixed values of λ. We observe that the optimal values for the x_{ijs} variables in the Lagrangian problem are given by

$$x_{ijs} = \begin{cases} y_j & \text{if } \lambda_{is} - c_{ij} \geq 0 \\ 0 & \text{otherwise} \end{cases} \quad . \tag{2.61}$$

Let us now define

$$R_j(\lambda) = \sum_{s=1}^{s^*} \sum_{i=1}^{n_s} \min(0, c_{ij} - \lambda_{is}) + f_j \quad , \tag{2.62}$$

and optimal values for y_j of (LAG_C) must solve

Objective

$$\min \sum_{j=1}^{m} R_j(\lambda) \cdot y_j \quad , \tag{2.63}$$

subject to

$$1 \leq \sum_{j=1}^{m} y_j \leq p \quad, \tag{2.64}$$

$$y_j \in \{0,1\} \quad j = 1,\ldots,m \quad. \tag{2.65}$$

Mostly, this problem is solved by a heuristic method, as a greedy heuristic, a dual ascent method, and so forth.

The lower bounds obtained by the proposed relaxation methods have a substantial impact on the efficiency of a branch-and-bound method.

Problem Selection

In Step 3 of the branch-and-bound algorithm we need to choose a subproblem IP_k which we want to examine next. We generally distinguish between *a priori rules* which determine in advance how the subproblems are to be developed and *adaptive rules* that use information about the status of the active problems. One widespread a priori rule is the LIFO (last in, first out) strategy, where $\mathcal{T}$ is stored as a stack. A current problem which is not removed is appended at the end of the list. The next problem to be examined is one of its two sons. This is a completely a priori rule, if we determine that the left son is considered before the right son and fix a rule for branching. If a problem is removed from $\mathcal{T}$, we go back on the path from this node to the root until we find the first father problem with an unexplored son. This strategy is also called *depth-first search*, since the search tree tends to get deeper quickly. Another strategy is the FIFO (first in, first out) rule, where we store $\mathcal{T}$ as a priority queue. A current problem which is not removed is put at the end of the queue and the problem at the first queue position will be considered next. This method creates broad search trees rather than deep trees and is therefore also called *breadth-first search*. An adaptive rule is, for instance, the LLB strategy (least lower bound). Again, we store $\mathcal{T}$ as a priority queue with respect to the lower bounds z_*. The next problem to be considered is the one with the least value of z_*. The latter methods will be the one we adopt for the solution of the COSYC problem, since from the problem structure we may assume that the problem with least lower bound may lead to an optimal solution faster than a problem selected by an a priori fixed rule. Alternatively, one could also use a heap structure to store $\mathcal{T}$ under a

LLB strategy.

Division

In step 5 of the algorithm, we divide a considered problem which has not been removed from $\mathcal{T}$ into two sons (subproblems). If we use a LP relaxation at each node this is simply done by adding linear constraints. A common strategy is to take $Y = Y_1 \cup Y_2$ with $Y_1 = Y \cap \{y \in \mathcal{R}_+^m \,|\, g \cdot y \leq g_0\}$ and $Y_2 = Y_k \cap \{y \in \mathcal{R}_+^m \,|\, g \cdot y \geq g_0 + 1\}$ with a $g \in \mathcal{Z}_+^m$ and $g_0 \in \mathcal{Z}_+$. If y_0 is the solution of the strong LP relaxation corresponding to Y and solution z_{LP}, we can choose (g, g_0) such that $g_0 < g \cdot y_0 < g_0 + 1$ which yields $y_0 \notin conv(Y_1) \cup conv(Y_2)$. Therefore, we might obtain $z_{1,LP}, z_{2,LP} > z_{LP}$ and we could remove one branch. The open question is now how to choose g and g_0. It may be desirable to split problem Y on a "important" variable y_j, rather than on an "unimportant" one. The importance of a y_j could for instance be expressed in form of dual information on the shadow prices. Splitting on the y_j with the largest shadow price may have the largest impact on the objective function of the primal problem. However, obtaining dual information may be too expensive in terms of computation time. It is cheaper to use information which is already available, i.e. from the solution of the LP relaxation of the father node. Let x_{ijs}^0 denote the optimal distributions of the y_j's from the LP relaxation with optimal value z_{LP}. Let

$$g_j = \sum_{s=1}^{s^*} \sum_{i=1}^{n_s} x_{ijs}^0 \quad . \tag{2.66}$$

A y_j variable may be called important, if its assigned number of cars is larger than the average. Hence, we define

$$g = t \cdot \sum_{s=1}^{s^*} \sum_{i=1}^{n_s} d_{is} \quad , \tag{2.67}$$

where $t \in [0; 1]$ characterizes a certain fraction of overall demand. t roughly determines the cardinality of Y_1 and Y_2. Choosing t too large or too small may result in "unbalanced" divisions. Small sets Y_1, for example, can probably be removed quickly from $\mathcal{T}$, since $z_{1,LP} > z_{LP}$, but $card(Y_2)$ gets smaller too slowly to achieve a change in $z_{2,LP}$.

Summing up, branch-and-bound methods utilizing relaxation methods seem to be an appropriate solution tool for moderately sized COSYC problems. However, since

m increases exponentially with the number of options q, the quality of lower bounds must improve similarly to obtain a tractable method. We will comment more detailed on the performance of branch-and-bound methods in section 2.7.

2.6.2 Column Generation

The major drawback of the branch-and-bound method was that each set of feasible solution vectors y of COSYC could once be considered as a node of the tree. The decomposition principle of Dantzig and Wolfe (1960) showed for the first time how large-scale linear programs with angular coefficient matrix can be solved very efficiently by decomposing it into a master program with only few rows but many columns and subproblems which generate only those column which are needed by the simplex method and returns them to the master program. This method is called "column generation". The resulting algorithm can be viewed as an iteration between a set of decoupled, and hence independent, subproblems whose objective functions contain variable parameters, and the master program. They receive a set of variables (i.e. simplex multipliers) from the master program and send their solutions back to the master program which combines these with previous solutions in an optimal way and computes new multipliers. The economic interpretation is that the master program coordinates the actions of the subproblems by setting prices and resources used by these problems.

Consider the LP

$$z_{LP} = \min\{cy \mid Ay \leq b, y \geq 0\} \quad . \tag{2.68}$$

Let y_0 be a basic feasible solution of length m with basis matrix B_0 and corresponding cost c_0. The simplex multipliers associated with the basis are $\pi = c_0 B_0^{-1}$. A basic feasible solution is improved by pricing out all columns corresponding to non-basic variables. For this purpose, $c^* = c - \pi A$ are the reduced cost coefficients. If $\min_j c_j = c_s^* < 0$ then, assuming non-degeneracy, the current solution may be improved by introducing y_s into the basis via a pivot transformation. Obviously, if m is large, this process gets very tedious. Frequently, the set of all columns has a well-defined structure in large-scale LPs. An example is the cutting stock problem (see section

2.2.1), in which all columns consist of non-negative integers and satisfy a linear coupling inequality.

We assume now that all columns a_j of LP are drawn from a set S which is typically the set of all m vectors satisfying some system of equations or inequalities. The column which enters the basis may be chosen by solving the subproblem

$$\min\{c(a_j) - \pi a_j \,|\, p_j \in S\} \quad . \tag{2.69}$$

The structure of S and c determines which technique may be used to solve (2.69), for example dynamic programming in the cutting-stock case. To obtain a similar technique for the COSYC problem we start with a feasible solution of COSYC with $p + 1$ harness types. We could use the q mandatory harnesses plus the $p - q + 1$ harness types which exactly correspond to the $p - q + 1$ car types with largest demand. Solving this moderately sized problem with branch-and-bound for instance, at least one harness type j' exists with $y_{j'} = 0$ due to the p-median constraint (2.38) which we call non-basic. The variable with the least reduced costs will be exchanged with a new harness type j^* generated by a suitable subproblem. For this purpose, we extend our notation as follows:

Auxiliary Variables:

$$v_{is} \;=\; \text{dual price of car } (i, s) \text{ for constraint (2.36).}$$
$$c_r \;=\; \text{unit cost of option } r.$$
$$h_{isr} \;=\; \begin{cases} 1 & \text{if car } (i, s) \text{ requires option } r. \\ 0 & \text{otherwise} \end{cases} .$$

Solution Variables:

$$w_{is} \;=\; \begin{cases} 1 & \text{if new harness satisfies car } (i, s). \\ 0 & \text{otherwise} \end{cases} .$$
$$z_r \;=\; \begin{cases} 1 & \text{if new harness includes option } r. \\ 0 & \text{otherwise} \end{cases} .$$

We can now define the following column generating SUBPROBLEM:

Objective

$$\min \sum_{r=1}^{q} c_r z_r - \sum_{s=1}^{s^*} \sum_{i=1}^{n_s} v_{is} w_{is} \quad , \tag{2.70}$$

subject to

$$w_{is} \cdot h_{isr} \leq z_r \quad r = 1, \ldots, q, \ s = 1, \ldots, s^*, \ i = 1, \ldots, n_s \quad , \tag{2.71}$$

$$w_{is}, z_r \in \{0, 1\} \quad r = 1, \ldots, q, \ s = 1, \ldots, s^*, \ i = 1, \ldots, n_s \quad . \tag{2.72}$$

In the objective function, we want to minimize the reduced cost of the new harness type which is generated, according to (2.69). Constraint (2.71) assures that the decision variable z_r must be set to one, if both the harness is meant to satisfy car (i, s) and car (i, s) requires option r.

The only problem which arises with the above formulation is that we must assume additivity of our cost structure, i.e., the cost of the new harness equals the sum of independent single option costs. We know from earlier considerations that this is in general not true, since our variable cost structure is non-additive, not even sub- or super-additive. However, sub-additivity does not hurt our procedure because we compute costs conservatively in (2.71) and may adjust them before we continue with the optimization of the COSYC master problem. If the super-additive effect in the volume-dependent cost is substantial, the cost of the new harness pattern may increase so much in the adjustment phase that it will not improve the solution of the COSYC problem anymore. Hence, we have to slightly change our cost structure in order to attain a well-behaved cost function. Moreover, fix costs for the new harness are not known in general and have to be estimated.

The complete column generating algorithm can now be stated:

Step 1 (Initialize):
Find a feasible set $\{y_1, \ldots, y_{p+1}\}$ for COSYC and let $z_* = \infty$.

Step 2 (Solve Master):
Find optimal value z_C of COSYC and dual prices v_{is}. Let $J^0 = \{j \leq p+1 | y_j = 0\}$.

Step 3 (Optimality Check):

If $z_C < z_*$ then let $z_* = z_C$ and go to step 5.

If $z_C \geq z_*$ let $J^0 = J^0 - j^*$. If $J^0 \neq \emptyset$, go to step 7.

Step 4 (Terminate or Loop):

If $J^0 = \emptyset$, then terminate with optimal value z_C of COSYC.

Step 5 (Solve Subproblem):

Solve SUBPROBLEM using the v_{is} variables. Let the resulting new harness pattern $y_z = (z_1, \ldots, z_q)$.

Step 6 (Adjust Costs):

Adjust volume- and variant-dependent costs of y_z.

Step 7 (Price out):

Choose $j^* \in J^0$ to be exchanged with y_z and go to step 2.

From J^0, we could choose indices j according to their reduced costs which may stem from an LP relaxation of COSYC or use other order criteria. As we furthermore see, the number of constraints in the COSYC problem has reduced significantly because we do not consider more than $p + 1$ harnesses for the master problem. The number of SUBPROBLEM constraints is independent of the number of potential harness candidates.

Since the objective value of COSYC has improved after at least $card(J^0)$ calls of the SUBPROBLEM or the algorithm has terminated, we will find the best solution after a finite number of steps. However, we have to be satisfied with a near optimal result, if our cost structure is non-additive. We will comment on the performance of the above column generation approach for real-world examples in section 2.7.

2.6.3   Simulated Annealing

Simulated annealing has been of recent interest for obtaining "good" solutions for a considerable variety of problems (see Connolly, 1992, or Collins, Eglese and Golden,

1988, for instance). The procedure is essentially derived from thermodynamics and tries to prevent a search scheme from getting stuck in local optima. The solution method accepts "uphill" steps of size δE (energy increase) with a probability $e^{-\delta E/T}$, where T signifies the temperature of the system. During the cooling process of the system, these uphill steps become less and less likely.

Similar to the idea utilized for the column generating subproblem (2.70)-(2.72), simulated annealing helps to design one new harness which enters the optimal harness set $\mathcal{H}$. For this purpose, we start with an initial harness design and try to improve it by pursuing the following local search scheme inspired by simulated annealing:

Step 1 (Initialize):
Define initial harness H with design $(z_1, \ldots, z_q)$. Let $z_* = \infty$, counter $k = 1$ and stop criterion $\epsilon <<$. Let initial temperature $T = 1$ and let geometric cooling coefficient $\alpha < 1$.

Step 2 (Terminate or Loop):
If $T < \epsilon$, then terminate with maximum cost decrease c_S.

Step 3 (Local Search):
Next option shift $r = k \bmod q$. Let $z_r = 1 - z_r$.

Step 4 (Solve Assignment Problem):
Find minimum harness cost z_S by assigning harness set $\mathcal{H} \cup H$ to cars. Let $\delta E = z_S - z_*$.

Step 5 (Optimality Check):
If $\delta E < 0$ then let $\mathcal{H} = \mathcal{H} \cup H$ and $z_* = z_S$. Goto Step 7.

Step 6 (Uphill Step):
$\beta = \text{RANDOM}(0;1)$. If $e^{-\delta E/T} > \beta$ then let $\mathcal{H} = \mathcal{H} \cup H$ and $z_* = z_S$.

Step 7 (Cooling):

Let $T = \alpha \cdot T$ and $k = k + 1$. Goto Step 2.

A neighborhood of a harness $\mathcal{H}$ is hence defined as all harnesses that can be obtained by shifting one value z_r. A neighbor is randomly chosen without replacement. If its cost is less than that of the incumbent, then it is accepted as the new incumbent. If its cost is greater, then it is accepted with a certain probability (see Corollary 4) to prevent the local search scheme from getting stuck in a poor local optimum. This procedure is repeated $\lceil \ln(\epsilon/T) / \ln(\alpha) \rceil + 1$ times until the algorithm stops.

Corollary 4: Given β, E. Then, the probability of an uphill step at any iteration step k with current temperature T_k is

$$\max\{0, 1 - \beta/T_k\} \quad .$$

Proof: From the procedure we know, that a cooling step is performed, if $\exp^{-E \cdot T_k} > \beta$. This holds for all values of E within the interval $[0; -T_k \cdot \ln(\beta)]$. Applying this to the corresponding density function yields the probability for an uphill step of

$$\int_0^{-T_k \cdot \ln(\beta)} \exp^{-E/T_k} dE \quad .$$

Straightforward integration proves the result.   □

In the next section, we will present a heuristic solution method, where the above procedure can be used to iteratively generate new harness designs.

2.6.4   A Greedy Closed Heuristic

The motivating idea for a heuristic is to avoid the already discussed drawbacks of either implicitly considering all possible harness types, or limiting oneself to an idealized additive cost structure. Therefore, we try to exploit the special structure of the problem. We start with a fairly large number of harnesses $m' > p$ which form a near-optimal solution, if variant-dependent costs are neglected. Then, we go backwards: the quantity of harnesses is continuously reduced by considering those pairs of harnesses (*parents*) which cause the largest marginal costs. From these parent harnesses we generate a *child* harness with an improved design and exchange it for its parents in the harness list. We shall proceed by this fashion until the number of harnesses drops below $p + 1$, and the overall cost function attains a minimum.

The initial harness set can be obtained by performing a Pareto analysis: we collect those high volume car variants of each considered car scenario which add up to a certain percentage (say 90%) of the entire car scenario volume and design the exactly corresponding harnesses as an initial set. Let m' denote the overall number of these car variants. Of course, one could use *all* different considered car variants as an optimal harness set, but their number is frequently greater than 25,000. Examinations of real world car type forecasts show, that one usually deals with a 90-10 distribution which means that 10 % of high-volume car variants contribute to 90 % of overall car volume. By deleting the redundant car variants which to a large amount occur in several car scenarios, one frequently ends up with

$$m' \approx \frac{1}{100} \cdot \sum_{s=1}^{s^*} n_s \quad . \tag{2.73}$$

The greedy heuristic thus can be described as follows:

Step 1 (Initialize):
Find a feasible set $I = \{1, \ldots, m'\}$ for COSYC. Let z_{j_1, j_2} be the optimal solution of COSYC for $I' = I - \{j_1, j_2\}$, if I' is feasible, and $z_{j_1, j_2} = \infty$, if I' is no feasible solution. Let $\bar{z} = \infty$.

Step 2 (Identify parent harnesses):
Find $\{j_1, j_2\} \subseteq I$ such that $z_{j_1, j_2} = \min\{z_{v,w} \mid \{v, w\} \subseteq I\}$.

Step 3 (Create child harness):
Generate a set J of new harness patterns from j_1 and j_2. For $j \in J$, let z_j be the solution of COSYC with respect to $I = I - \{j_1, j_2\} \cup \{j\}$.

Step 4 (Find "fittest" child):
Let $z^* = \min\{z_j \,|\, j \in J\}$ and corresponding fittest child pattern j^*. Let $I = I - \{j_1, j_2\} \cup \{j^*\}$ and $i_C = card(I)$.

Step 5 (Terminate or Loop):
If $i_C > p$ then go to step 2.
If $i_C \leq p$ then stop if $\bar{z} < z^*$. Else, let $\bar{z} = z^*$ and go to step 2.

In step 4, the cardinality of the index set I is successively reduced by one. If $card(I)$ drops below p for the first time, we start to store the minimum cost value achieved by the child/parent replacement procedure. The algorithm terminates, if z^* gets larger again than the prior optimal value $\bar{z}$. Here, we use the sub-modularity of our overall cost function which we have proved in section 2.6.3. Due to the underlying inherent binary conception and logic, it is convenient, to implement a harness as a bit sequence $(1101\ldots)$, indicating the respective option content. An appropriate method to create child harnesses from two parent harnesses is to vary the option content of a child pattern between the conjunction and the union of options of the parent harnesses. Since the parent harnesses may be substantially different with regard to their option content, we freely vary only a fixed number k_0 of options for reasons of computation time. Alternatively, we could use the simulated annealing heuristic of section 2.6.3 to attain an optimal "bit-shifting" during the child harness generation phase.

The time effort of step 2 is clearly a $\mathcal{O}(i_C^2)$. The effort of step 4 is limited by $\mathcal{O}(2^{k_0})$. Hence, the overall performance of the above greedy heuristic is in the worst case

$$\mathcal{O}\left(2^{k_0} * \sum_{j=2}^{m'} j^2\right) \,, \tag{2.74}$$

or a $\mathcal{O}(2^{k_0} * m'^3)$ and is thus significantly faster than an enumeration procedure for "reasonable" values k_0.

In the next section, we will assess strengths and weaknesses of either solution strategy, utilizing experimental data and real problem datasets from the automobile industry.

2.7 Computational Results

In the first part of this section, we demonstrate the behavior of each method for real problems. Therefore, we have selected current data from three technical components of a German automobile manufacturer. In the second part of this section, we will conduct some numerical experiments with the three methods described in section 2.6 based on randomly generated input data.

2.7.1 Application to Selected Components

The first problem we look at is to determine the physical design, power capacity and number of *car batteries*. On one hand, the minimum required power capacity of a battery is determined by some few options as air conditioning, power steering, and so forth. On the other hand, the physical size of a battery which mainly impacts power capacity, is affected by the front end package of the car as well as by regional restrictions on crashworthiness properties. Originally, the worker at the line needed to handle seven different batteries with capacity from 40 to 70 Ah. The cost structure of the battery problem is subadditive.

The second problem is to optimally design *steering column* types. The technical features and designs of steering columns are driven by options as power steering, driver airbag, tilt/telescope capabilities, and so forth. Initially, 12 different steering column designs were dealt with. The cost structure of the steering column problem is subadditive.

The third problem is to optimize a full *body wiring harness* with regard to its option wire content (see sections 2.3, 2.5 and 2.6). The initial number of body harnesses for the concerning car model was 41. As we know, the wiring harness cost structure is not subadditive.

The three problem sizes and cost structures differ substantially (see table 2.3), and we have furthermore assessed different values of p. The three methods (see sections

2.6.1, 2.6.2 and 2.6.4) have been implemented in FORTRAN on a CRAY Y-MPS. For the branch-and-bound method, we took the initial scenario as a feasible solution and obtained a lower bound by solving the problem with zero fix costs. To improve the bounds, we solve the Lagrangian dual problem with an ascent method similar to the one proposed in Cornuejols, Fisher and Nemhauser (1977). The branch-and-bound procedure was implemented as a heap employing an adaptive least lower bound strategy for the subproblem selection. For our greedy algorithm, we chose the generic-type heuristic to generate new component designs. Since from a practical standpoint we are mainly interested in reducing our total costs with respect to the initial component variety and design, we use the following performance measure:

$$PM = \frac{\text{initial cost} - \text{least cost found}}{\text{initial cost}} \quad . \tag{2.75}$$

Table 2.3 summarizes the performance of each tested method with regard to CPU time and quality of result for each test problem. As one sees, for the moderately

Figure 2.3: Problem Size and Solution Times

Problem	Parameters			Branch&Bound		Column Gen.		Greedy Closed	
	n	q	p	PM	Sec.	PM	Sec.	PM	Sec.
Battery	144	8	4	0.063	2.99	0.063	3.74	0.063	3.14
			6	0.188	6.11	0.188	5.15	0.187	2.88
			8	-0.011	9.38	-0.011	7.93	-0.014	2.41
Steering	4,143	16	8	-0.195	248.2	-0.195	38.45	-0.203	28.31
Column			12	0.145	444.8	0.145	119.9	0.141	21.89
			16	-0.093	716.2	-0.093	213.1	-0.095	17.17
Body	25,223	52	20	-	> 28,800	-0.141	2,434	-0.122	3,099
Wiring			40	-	> 28,800	0.296	3,127	0.345	2,611
Harness			60	-	> 28,800	0.032	3,641	0.144	2,329

sized battery problem, all three algorithms produce almost the same results, and computation times do not vary significantly. Hence, using 6 optimized battery designs instead of the current 7 designs yields a total cost decrease of almost 19 %. For the large scale steering column problem, computation time for the branch-and-bound method has rapidly grown. The column generation method shows the same results within less than a third of time effort. The greedy heuristic is substantially quicker than both other methods. However, the integrality gap of the greedy results is approximately 3%. For the huge scale harness problem, the greedy heuristic could not find the optimal result within 8 hours of CPU time. The greedy heuristic terminated within less than one hour of CPU and improved the initial cost by 34.5% for 40 optimized instead of 41 non-optimized harnesses. The computation times of the column generation approach are similar to the greedy times, the quality of the results, however, has worsened remarkably. This can essentially be attributed to the non-subadditivity of the harness cost structure.

For moderately sized problems, branch-and-bound methods have turned out to produce optimal results in reasonable time. For large scale problems with additive or at least subadditive costs, the column generation algorithm works very efficiently with close-to-optimal results. In the case of non-subadditive costs and many candidate component designs, the greedy closed heuristic is the best tradeoff between CPU time and quality of results.

2.7.2 Numerical Experiments

In this section, we want to study the impact of changes in demand, factory span, and option variety on the performance measure (2.75) introduced in the last section. For this purpose, we have randomly generated a disaggregated option-based car scenario of $n = 1,000$ car types, $q = 20$ options considered, and a maximum factory span of $p = 10$ component types. The underlying cost structure is random too, but strictly sub-additive. Fix costs are assumed constant for each component type.

We have characterized a change in demand or forecast horizon as a change in the number of different car types n, since reduced forecast horizon or more focused demand always means a decrease of car scenarios, and vice versa. A change of factory span, i.e., a expansion or reduction of floor storage space, is represented by a change in variable p. Eventually, a manufacturer's change in option variety is expressed in terms of changes of q. On a scale of -25% to 25%, we have randomly perturbed n, p and q in our car data base in steps of 5%. In order to even out the "bias of randomness" in our perturbations, we have processed 10 random perturbations at each step which resulted in 330 optimization runs for each of the three methods assessed. For each perturbation, the initial set of component designs consisted of the $p - 1$ high-runner variants which contributed to the most frequent car types plus one "super component" which ensures feasibility of the initial design. In the sensitivity results which can be seen in Figures 2.4 to 2.6, we have characterized the mean performance measure of the ten perturbations at each step. Although all results have been computed as discrete values at each perturbation step, we have expanded them to continuous curves to improve the visual interpretation.   PM

Figure 2.4: Sensitivity With Respect to Changes in Demand

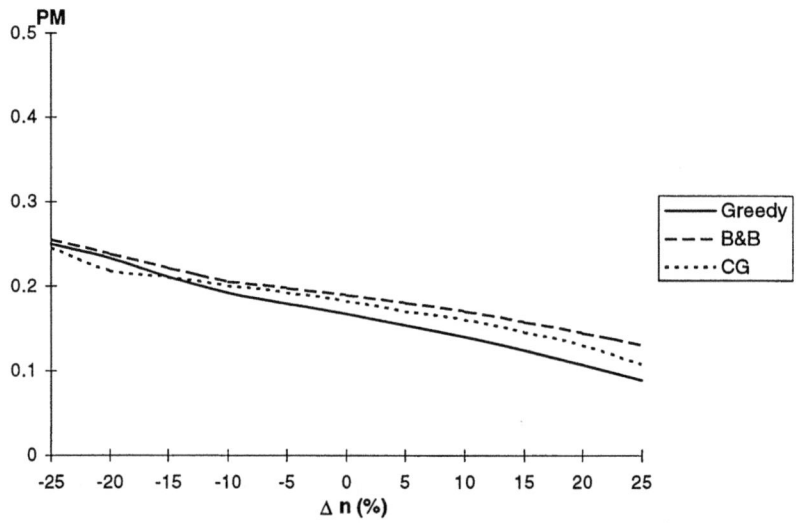

has proved to be very sensitive with respect to changes of all three parameters. If demand gets more certain or the forecast horizon gets shorter (Figure 2.4), our objective function can be generally decreased, i.e., costs are reduced. If we are dealing with many scenarios or car types due to uncertain forecasts or dispersed demand, costs go up. For a small number of car types, all three methods produce almost the same result. As n increases, the branch-and-bound method turns out to be superior to the column generation approach, the greedy heuristic comes off worst. Interestingly, the column generation method turns out to be inferior to both

Figure 2.5: Sensitivity With Respect to Changes in Factory Span

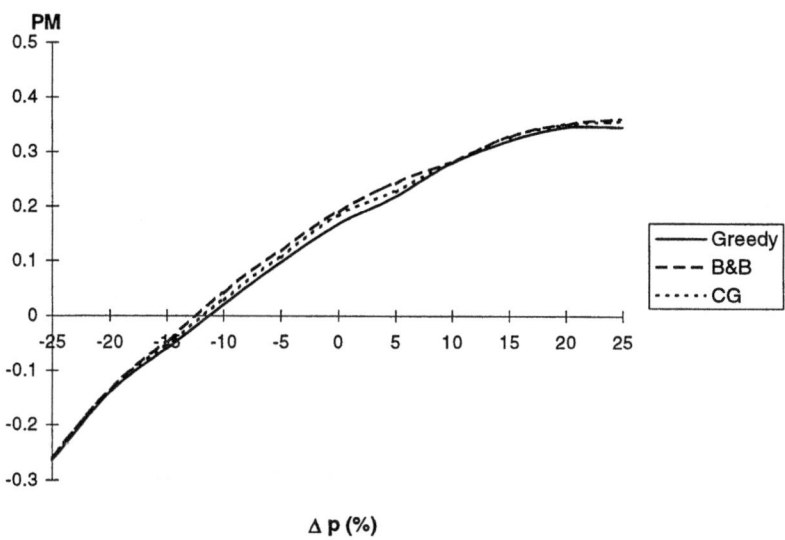

other methods for a perturbation level of -20% to -15% and catches up again for larger values of n. The reason for this is a significant sub-additive cost effect in the solution of both, branch-and-bound and greedy heuristic at this perturbation level. The column generation method was not able to reflect this effect of economies of scope in its own optimal component design due to the additivity assumption which underlies the column generation concept (see section 2.6.2).

In Figure 2.5, one sees the effect, if, for instance, storage space at the line is increased or reduced, i.e., the number p of allowed component designs changes. In general, the branch-and-bound method comes off best again, the greedy heuristic comes off worst. However, the differences are not substantial. p turns out to be the most sensitive parameter examined, PM varies between -.26 and .36 in the described perturbation range. For $p = 8$ or less, we are already better off with the initial "common-sense" solution of 10 components. Unlike Figure 2.4, the resulting curves are globally concave with a maximum for $p = 12$. If p gets larger than 12, the number of optimal components does not increase anymore due to the high fix costs associated with each additional design.

Figure 2.6: Sensitivity With Respect to Changes in Option Variety

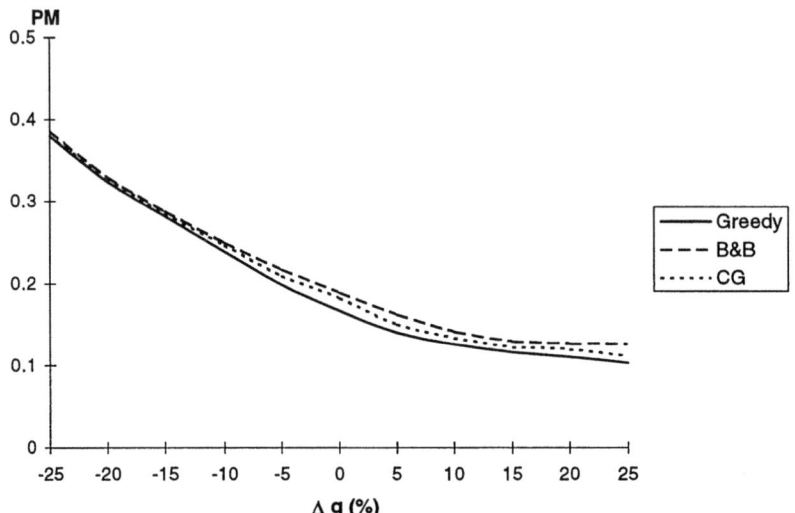

If we cut down or expand the range of our option offer (see Figure 2.6), in terms of q, we clearly reduce or increase our overall costs, respectively. Again, the greedy heuristic shows worse results than the branch-and-bound method and the column generation approach, whereas the differences are not as significant as in Figure 2.4. The results from the ten sample car scenarios at each perturbation step showed the highest variance among all parameter studies. The reason is that the optimization results not only depend on the number of additional or reduced options, but also on the associated option costs which were also generated as random. Therefore, the convex character of the curves in Figure 2.6 can not be generalized. We found some admittedly "pathological" examples where global convexity was violated. In most cases, however, the local convexity claim can be retained.

Finally, we want to demonstrate the trade-off accuracy of results versus computation time. From our above findings, the results obtained by the branch-and-bound method are best. The column generation method comes off second, at least if the cost structure is additive, with more or less marginal advantages over the greedy heuristic. In Figure 2.7, we have given the bounds on CPU time for each method and each parameter study. The branch-and-bound method requires approximately

Figure 2.7: Bounds on CPU Times

Varied Parameter	Branch-and-Bound lower/upper bound CPU time (sec)	Column Generation lower/upper bound CPU time (sec)	Greedy lower/upper bound CPU time (sec)
n	282 - 331	66 - 91	21 - 27
p	194 - 427	62 - 121	20 - 27
q	216 - 434	51 - 130	16 - 41

ten times the CPU time of the greedy heuristic, the column generation method approximately three times as much. As one can see, the magnitude of the CPU time prevalently depends on p and q, rather than on n for most of the methods.

As we already noted in the section before, the efficiency of either method strongly depends on the problem size. For the above medium sized random test problem, our greedy heuristic has proven to be significantly faster than all other methods with only marginal loss in accuracy of the results.

2.8   Summary

In this chapter, we have demonstrated how a car manufacturer can minimize the cost for a wide range of typical car components. We have motivated the problem, and we have surveyed the related literature. Moreover, we have characterized all cost factors, including the cost of complexity, which are essential to obtain a complete cost structure. Since our optimization approach is based on future demand, we have shown how current sales data can be combined with option or option combination forecasts to obtain a highly disaggregated description of future sales by a linear programming approach. However, we have emphasized that this car type data base does not include lost-sales data and therefore does not perfectly describe future customer preferences.

Subsequently, we have introduced the formulation of a stochastic mixed-integer program which allows to minimize overall component costs by determining their optimal designs and the optimal number of different designs. Since the mixed-integer program has many constraints, traditional solution methods are not suited for realistic problem sizes. For this reason, we have formally analyzed three potential solution methods, i.e., a traditional branch-and-bound method, a column generation approach, and a new greedy heuristic based on a genetic-type algorithm or simulated annealing, alternatively.

All three methods have been implemented and tested with real data from a German car manufacturer. Furthermore, we have studied the impact of small perturbations in the initial key data on the quality of results and the computation time for each of the three methods. We found out that the choice of the "right" method is strongly problem-dependent. For small problems, the branch-and-bound method renders the best results, and computation times do not differ a lot among all methods. For larger problems, the branch-and-bound method becomes intractable. In this case, we either recommend a column generation approach, as long as the cost structure is additive, or the greedy method otherwise. We have empirically shown that changes of demand, of production capacity or of option supply can tremendously affect the optimal solution. We therefore recommend this optimization procedure to be carried out at least each model year to capitalize on potential cost savings due to changes in the market or production environment.

Chapter 3

Option Bundling And Bundle Pricing

3.1 Motivation And Framework

Bundling is the widespread practice of offering a number of products or services in a single package at an "attractive" price. A bundle can be viewed as a new product, where the differentiation from existing products is achieved by deciding upon three crucial factors:

- the composition of the bundle

- the bundle price

- the form of bundling.

However, bundling has some important advantages over designing a new single product. First, it starts with already available information on production and market conditions. This significantly reduces the high costs associated with a conventional product development and consequently decreases the risk of failure when a new product is brought to the market. Furthermore, bundling provides a relatively cheap opportunity to enhance differentiation from competitors and can contribute to a positive public image. The potential profitability of bundling is mainly due to two sources. First, fix costs plus variable costs of a bundle may be substantially lower than the sum of the costs for the individual items (sub-additive cost function). These costs may consist of setup and holding costs in the manufacturing industry, as well as order processing and administrative costs in the service industry. Second, from the market side, bundling can be viewed as a tool to discriminate between customers with heterogeneous tastes, as well as a possibility to sell divisible goods at higher margins to consumers with strong specific tastes. Bundle pricing allows the vendor to move a step closer to the dream of every marketer, namely, value based pricing, that is, charge each customer his/her value received for his/her purchase.

In the next sections we will focus on the three cornerstones of bundling mentioned above. Although an optimal strategy requires a simultaneous decision on form, composition and pricing of a bundle, we will first investigate the specific aspects of each factor. Subsequently, examples and a comprehensive literature review will be provided in section 3.2.

In section 3.3, we address the potential implications of option bundling for an automobile manufacturer. We will show that it is advantageous when market, manufacturing and competition aspects are considered simultaneously, rather than limiting the effects of bundling to either cost savings or demand stimulation.

In section 3.4, we will focus on the theoretical aspects of bundling. The main contribution of this paper is to develop a mathematical model, which provides a management tool to decide upon the profitability of several bundling strategies. The model is hereby able to map the random distribution of customer demand. This includes reservation prices for single products and bundles, as well as "cannibalization" effects which may occur among products of one product line, several product lines or even different car brands. We combine marketing and manufacturing data and develop an algorithm using conjoint analysis and mathematical programming tools to determine bundle composition and bundle prices under uncertainty. In particular, we emphasize the implementation of the presented approach for an automobile manufacturer. We show, how to obtain the necessary input data, i.e., find the mean and the variance of the a priori unknown demand distributions as well as a measure for the randomness of choice behavior, in an inexpensive and efficient way, using internally available resources. By establishing a continuous information flow, the presented optimization approach can be applied in a very flexible way which enables the car manufacturer to quickly react to changes in demand and production conditions.

A heuristic solution method for the hard stochastic bundle pricing problem is presented in section 3.5. It is based on decomposing the problem appropriately. We furthermore present a path-following technique which helps to bypass the problem of getting stuck in poor local optima during the optimization.

In section 3.6 we will test the presented methodology by solving a large-scale problem from the automobile industry, check the sensitivity of the model with respect to the demand structure and "translate" results and other gained experience into useful rules-of-thumb for early management decisions.

3.1.1 The Composition of the Bundle

A bundle can consist of two or more products or services which may have complementary or substitutive character. In general, there does not seem to exist a general distinction between both terms (see section 3.2).

From a production point of view, bundling should be encouraged among components that have high setup costs to benefit from economies of scope. In car manufacturing, an important option cost driver which can be used as an indicator for sub-additive costs, is the wiring harness (see chapter 1). Most of the door options as power door lock, mirror, and windows, burglar alarm and radio use require an expensive door plug which is installed in the car's A-pillar and connects each door wire with the corresponding switches and devices in the dashboard. This plug has to be installed, if one of the mentioned electrical options is contained in the car, and can subsequently be used by all of them. Thus, marginal harness costs for the second, third, etc. door option only consist of the material costs for the additional wires and slightly increased labor effort. In general, we can achieve lower marginal costs for bundles, if the manufacturing costs of the individual items are sub-additive.

Other manufacturing issues which may benefit from a reasonable bundling concept are line balancing, production smoothing, and capacity utilization. For a car manufacturer, labor intensive options as a passenger airbag with production share between 30 and 70% can be critical, in particular, if many workstations are involved in the assembly process. If the job load changes significantly at a workstation in final assembly for each second or third car, this automatically leads to frequent idle times of workers, as well as reduced capacity utilization of machines. By option bundling, one can achieve a controlled increase (or decrease) of the production share of certain options which provides an opportunity to re-balance jobs and even out workload. We will address these aspects in more detail in section 3.2. Another important opportunity which arises using the bundling strategy, is deproliferation (see section 3.1.3).

On the demand side, the main idea of offering a collection of components as opposed to sell them individually is similar to the idea of price promotions: a bundle will increase profit, if the usual discount (see section 3.1.2) is outweighed by the additional demand for the package. Market expansion is a key factor of bundling (Eppen, Hanson and Martin; 1991). To increase demand, it is necessary to understand which elements of the product line are valued by the consumers (see examples 1 and 2, section 3.1.3).

The choice of the "ingredients" of a bundle for instance enables the marketer to design a bundle for various customer segments which have a large intersection of valued single items: for three items A, B and C we may have a segment which strongly prefers items A and C, another one values B and C. By attractively pricing bundle ABC, we may achieve that both segments will purchase it. Especially in the car industry, hierarchical bundles are used to create a trade-up effect: the car's trim levels usually start with a basic car with little standard features. Subsequent trim levels are defined by successively adding equipment to the last trim level. The idea is to persuade a customer to "trade up" to the next trim level. Eppen, Hanson and Martin (1991) suggest that the number of trade-up bundles generally is determined by demand: "... strong demand favors few offerings and more of a pure bundling approach. Weak demand favors more alternatives with smaller gaps between bundles."

An important aspect of bundling in service industries is to make it unattractive for the customer to switch brands by reducing customers transaction costs and raising switching costs. A variety of American banks already use bundled accounts which comprise credit cards, checking accounts, certificates of deposit, and loans. The convenience of customers of doing all their banking with one institution is one of the biggest selling points used to push the bundled accounts. Customers with bundled accounts also tend to commit larger sums of money (Radigan, 1992). As a side effect, bundled accounts reduce the overhead and support costs of taking in new deposits and making loans. A similar effect can be observed in cellular industry. AT&T, for instance, bundles long distance calls with domestic offerings at a discounted price, and thus significantly succeeds to reduce consumer trial and switching (Brown, 1992).

A crucial point of a bundling strategy is, whether the bundle concept succeeds in clearly defining the product (see section 3.2). A consumer, who is not familiar with a product or service, may need an overall idea of the intention of a particular bundle (e.g. a safety package in a car, consisting of dual airbags, ABS, traction control and a reinforced passenger cavity). Even, if a customer has no experience with traction control, he may feel safe to order it in the company of some well-known safety features.

As we will show in section 3.3, the question which products to bundle should not be decided "by gut-feel", but is a part of the overall optimization problem to design and price bundles to maximize profit.

3.1.2 The Bundle Price

In this subsection we want to describe the basic assumptions and mechanisms, which underlie optimal pricing methods for a particular bundling strategy. A quantitative assessment will be provided in section 3.3.

A widely used idea to describe demand is the concept of a customer's *reservation price*. We assume that each (potential) customer has a hypothetical maximum price which he is willing to pay for a product with certain attributes. If the product price is lower than a customer's reservation price, he will purchase it. A more formal derivation of reservation prices can be found in Kalish and Nelson (1988). They show that a consumer's reservation price for a product is equal to the total utility contribution of the product divided by the marginal utility of money. The (positive) difference between the customer's reservation price and the actual price of the product is called *consumer surplus*. We will assume that a customer purchases either one unit of a certain product or does not purchase anything. Thus, if a customer has several offers, he will choose the one which maximizes his personal surplus, a synonym for utility in this context.

Mostly in practice and theory, demand is not considered at the consumer level. Similar consumer preferences are accumulated to an aggregated reservation price of an entire *customer segment*. This deterministic approach assumes that the variance of consumers reservation prices within a segment is very small. We will drop this restrictive assumption in section 3.3 and consider reservation price as a stochastic variable. However, the deterministic approach is convenient to understand the "dynamics" of bundling. For the sake of reduced model complexity, it is completely sufficient for the quality of results, if "sharp" separation of customer segments is feasible.

In practice, one can observe that reservation prices are sub-additive which means that the reservation price for an entire component bundle is not greater than the sum of reservation prices for the single items. Of course, there exist exceptions from this rule. If a package of products increases their overall utility, as observed for collectible items, reservation price may be super-additive for these components. According to Lewbel (1985), a customer's reservation price will be sub-additive, if he perceives the bundled goods as substitutes and super-additive, if the goods are complementary. In general, a distinction between substitution and complementarity is often difficult. As Dansby and Conrad (1984) point out, the utility of a bundle can also be less than the sum of the individual items' reservation prices when certain restrictions are imposed on the use of the bundle. A travel package, consisting of air transportation and lodging, may only be available with some restrictions on the travel time.

Under the objective to maximize profit by optimally extracting consumer surplus, sub-additive reservation prices imply sub-additive product pricing. If a customer purchases a bundle of components, he usually gets a discount on the price of the single items. If costs are strictly additive, bundling reduces profit obtained by those customers, who would purchase all components individually. However, bundling may create additional demand, and thus profit, from consumers, who didn't purchase any component or purchased only some components of the bundle.

Profit increases and gains of market shares due to bundling may be substantial. Watson (1990) reports of IBM's tie-in sales in the early 30's (which relates to pure bundling, see section 3.1.3). IBM maintained a quasi-monopoly on tabulating machines and obliged their customers to purchase all punch cards, which were no IBM monopoly, from IBM. According to Sobel (1981), punch card sales – as a direct consequence of tabulator sales – contributed by almost 40% to IBM's overall annual revenues.

A recent example in the German micro-computer branch is Vobis Microcomputer AG. Their bundling strategy is considered to be an important factor of their market leadership. Due to high component modularity, each customer can build his own bundle which consists of CPU, monitor, printer software and additional hardware. A customer can even create his own system configuration, comprising base module (processor), VGA-card, hard disk and keyboard. Bundle discounts at Vobis generally range from 3 to 10%, and relatively increase with the bundle price.

We will show that for several typical distribution patterns, profit depending on price is a concave function, and that a globally profit-maximizing bundle price exists. Hanson and Martin (1991) present a mathematical approach how to obtain optimal bundle prices in the deterministic case (see also 3.1.4). We will present a method which also allows to consider the stochastic case.

3.1.3   The Form of Bundling

Besides *unbundled* sales, where no item is offered within a bundle, we distinguish between two different forms of bundling. In *pure bundling*, no component of the bundle is available individually. In *mixed bundling*, all components of the bundle can also be purchased as single items. A recent example of pure bundling is the ticket sales practice for the soccer world championships 1994 in the US. It was not possible to purchase first-round tickets for one particular event such as the opening match of Germany and Bolivia in Chicago. Tickets were only offered en bloc, comprising several matches for one location which lead to decent sales volumes even for the potentially unattractive matches (which did not prevent brokers to unbundle ticket packages and profit, however). Another example is block-booking in the movie industry. Instead of giving a theater owner the freedom to pick only the most attractive movies, often only combined assortments of movies are offered by the movie rental companies (Stigler, 1963, 1968).

In the service industry, maintenance contracts for computer hardware frequently consist of a variety of services which are not offered individually to the customer. A special case of pure bundling are tie-in sales, where the buyer of a tying good agrees to purchase any tied goods only from the distributor of the main product. The tying good mostly is a machine (computer, copier), the tied good is a required resource to run the machine (data discs, copy paper) (see also the IBM example of coupled tabulating machine and punch card sales, section 3.1.2).

It can also be considered as a form of bundling, if the same physical good is sold in different container sizes (or a service contract is offered for several time periods). Wholesale retailers (e.g. METRO) are frequently only offering a pallet with many bottles of the same detergent or durable goods in unusually large amounts. This special case of pure bundling is opposed to the well-known retail practice to offer, for instance, orange juice in many bottle sizes from 1/4 to 2 liters with quantity discounts, a form of mixed bundling.

A special form of mixed bundling is called *premium bundling* (Cready, 1991). Instead of selling bundles with a discount, they are charged with a premium relative to the prices of the individual items. Stamp collectors are willing to pay a higher price for a complete set of stamps than the prices of the single stamps would suggest (see 3.1.4).

Examples of mixed bundling can be encountered in almost every business branch. It is particularly common in service industry (Guiltinan, 1987). Banks offer credit cards at no annual fee and free traveler's checks for "special" customers. Insurances sell bundles consisting of liability plus accident insurance. Hotels are offering weekend packages that combine lodging and meals at special rates or restaurants attract their guests with lunch menus (starter, main course, desert and drink) at special rates. In health clubs, a customer can choose between individual programs (aerobic classes, weight room, sauna), packages combining several of these activities or a universal membership. Airlines bundle vacation packages (air travel, car rental, lodging) or offer frequent flyer programs, where a certain amount of accumulated flight miles means free round-trips for the passenger. The latter idea is closely related to couponing which can also be viewed as a form of mixed bundling. Discounts on a mixed bundle can occur in two forms (Guiltinan, 1987): in "mixed-joint form", there exists an explicit price for the bundle, in "mixed-leader form", the consumer obtains a discount on one product, if he purchases another product at a regular price.

A very important aspect of bundling in a production framework is deproliferation. In particular, pure bundling can ex ante reduce the product, and hence process variety to a large amount. If a pure bundle consists of m items with $2^m - 1$ possible combinations, the product variety is reduced by $k-1$, where $k \leq 2^m - 1$ is the number of feasible combinations of the m single items. This desired feature is not so obvious for mixed bundling. As long as all products in a bundle can still be purchased as single items, the number of possible product combinations is not reduced. However, achieving a large penetration for a mixed bundle by attractive prices for the bundle and increased prices for particular individual items, is practically equivalent to pure bundling. From a production point of view, especially these items should be excluded from the customers' choice of single products which have high cost synergies with other products in the bundle. Pure bundling obviously not only reduces product variety, but also decreases product variety for the customer.

In general, as Schmalensee (1984) points out, pure bundling reduces effective buyer heterogeneity by aiming at aggregated reservation prices (see 3.3). The strength of unbundled sales is the ability to collect high prices from consumers with extreme tastes. Mixed bundling combines the features of pure bundling and unbundled sales. In general, the decision on the form of bundling is a tradeoff, determined by cost and utility levels, as well as correlation of demand for the considered components.

It is straightforward to show that under the assumptions of non-negative reservation prices, pure bundling is a special case of mixed bundling, and can therefore never be more profitable. Selling a pure bundle at a price p_B and pricing the bundle at p_B in the mixed bundling case as well, yields the same distribution of goods among consumers, if single components are priced higher than p_B each (nobody will buy a single item). In practice however, mixed bundling is not generally more profitable than pure bundling. If non-negative reservation prices in fact exist, and we are not able to ask for arbitrarily high single component prices, fix costs for the individual items which we still have to produce, may be profit reducing. Under the assumption of additive costs $(c_1, \ldots, c_n)$ for n single items we can even price each single item below the bundle price p_B, namely $p_i = p_B + c_i - \sum_{k=1}^{n} c_k$ $(i = 1 \ldots n)$, such that the profit obtained by mixed bundling is identically the same as for the optimal pure bundling strategy.

McAfee, McMillan and Whinston (1989) show that for independently distributed preferences, (mixed) bundling always dominates unbundled sales. However, even under the fairly strong assumption of normally distributed demand (Schmalensee, 1984), there is no general rule, whether bundling is more profitable than unbundled sales. We want to illustrate the simple case of a two dimensional price space (two products), deterministic demand in form of perfect knowledge of customer segments and fixed reservation prices for each segment. The following example shows, that either mixed bundling or unbundled sales can be preferable for a given (discrete) distribution of reservation prices.

Example 1:

We consider four customer segments with symmetrically distributed and negatively

Figure 3.1: Negative Correlation of Reservation Prices

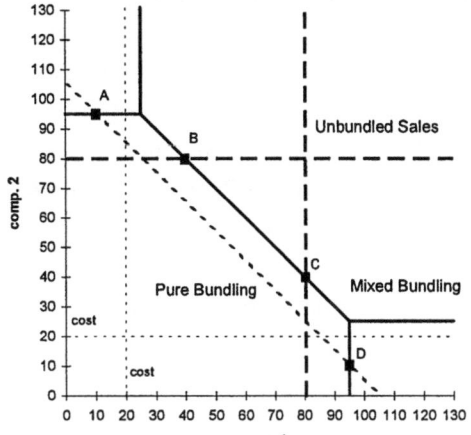

correlated reservation prices for A (10,95), B (40,80), C (80,40) and D (95,10). Costs for both components are set to (20,20) and 40 for the bundle. Figure 3.1 shows that under each strategy the reservation price space is split into several regions, four for unbundled sales and mixed bundling, two for pure bundling. For each pricing strategy we state the optimal individual prices p_1, p_2, the optimal bundle price p_B and the resulting overall profit Π below.

Pricing Strategy	p_1	p_2	p_B	profit
unbundled sales	80	80	–	240
pure bundling	–	–	105	260
mixed bundling	95	95	120	310

Demand for the bundle is very elastic, since its reservation prices only vary between 105 and 120 among all four customer segments. However, demand for the individual components varies between 10 (below cost) and 95. It seems reasonable, to prefer an unbundled sales strategy, if we only deal with extreme tastes as segments A and D, because consumer surplus can be completely extracted and profit margins are high. A complete extraction of consumer surplus in any bundling strategy would mean to lower profit margins, because the reservation prices for the less preferred items are below costs. Adding consumer segments B and C changes the situation. To include segments B and C in unbundled sales, we have to decrease price from 95 to 80 for each component which lowers margins. Including these segments in a pure bundling strategy leaves the optimal price of 105 unchanged, since the reservation prices $r(B), r(C)$ are greater than 105. However, consumer surplus can not be completely extracted anymore $(s(A) = s(D) = 0, s(B) = s(C) = 15)$. Mixed bundling is able to fully extract surplus of B and C by the bundle, as well as fully extract surplus of A and D by their preferred single components. Since the margin of the bundle is not much greater than for the single items, mixed bundling turns out to be most profitable in this example.

Example 2:

Figure 3.2: Positive Correlation of Reservation Prices

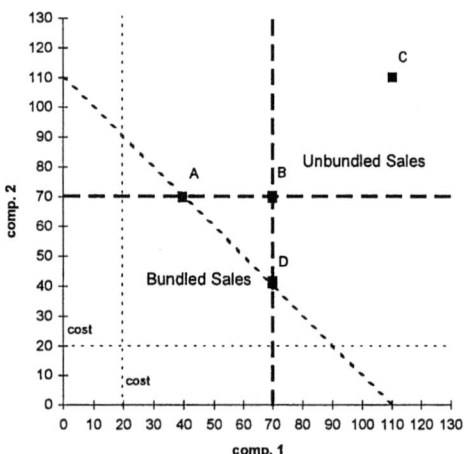

We now consider four customer segments with symmetrically distributed and positively correlated reservation prices, in particular for A (40,70), B (70,70), C (110,110) and D (70,40) (see Figure 3.2).

Optimal prices and resulting profit for costs (20,20) are now:

	p_1	p_2	p_B	profit
unbundled sales	70	70	–	300
pure bundling	–	–	110	280
mixed bundling	>70	>70	110	280

Demand for the bundle is inelastic now, reservation prices vary between 110 and 220 among the segments, and range from 40 to 110 for the single items. Considering only customer segments A and D, we would always prefer bundled sales, as opposed to unbundled sales: although consumer surplus can be completely extracted under both strategies, tying the less preferred single item in the bundle, raises margins. Adding segments B and C to the demand scenario does not change the optimal price for the bundled sales: gaps between the four bundle reservation prices are so large that no segment can be excluded without lowering profit. Consumer surplus cannot be sufficiently extracted anymore ($s(A) = s(D) = 0$, $s(B) = 30$, $s(C) = 110$). In the unbundled case, optimal prices don't change either, but the surplus of customer segment B can be fully extracted ($s(B) = 0$) and the surplus of segment C is lower than in the bundled case ($s(C) = 80$). This more than compensates the slightly higher margins in bundling. We also observe that in this case mixed bundling yields the same profit as pure bundling: individual items under mixed bundling have to be priced higher than 70, to exclude segments A and D from the less profitable single component purchase (a single component price of less than 70 would include them in both cases single purchase or bundle purchase, and they would choose the alternative, which maximizes their surplus). But then, on the other hand, surplus for each segment will always be maximum, if the entire bundle is purchased, thus no single component will be sold. Pure and mixed bundling are identical in this example.

In section 3.3 we will obtain general insights by numerical analysis on how demand distribution characteristics and the underlying cost structure in the n-dimensional case influence the decisions on the form of bundling.

3.2   Literature Review

Roughly speaking, the existing literature can be segmented into four groups:

- legal, political and welfare-related consequences
- competition related issues
- supportive market conditions
- economic analysis

However, a strict categorization does not seem to be possible due to the interrelationship of each field.

The earliest examinations in the economic literature on product bundling mainly assess antitrust and policy implications of bundling as a subtle price discrimination tool. Stigler (1963) addresses block-booking and demonstrates that a movie distributor can raise profits by leasing only combined packages of movies instead of individual movies. The underlying idea is to prevent the customer from selecting "attractive" movies only and ignore inferior ones. In his framework which represents the basis for many subsequent studies, demand is modeled by explicit customer segments with assigned reservation prices for each product. Each segment will always choose the surplus maximizing product. Reservation price and cost structure are assumed to be strictly additive. He concludes that (pure) bundling is profitable, if reservation prices are negatively correlated, while their aggregations (bundle reservation price) are similar for each segment.

In a related line of research, Burstein (1960), Telser (1965) and Stigler (1968) investigate tie-in sales which requires customers to purchase a commodity (tied good) with a focal product (tying good). In the IBM example of punch card sales tied to tabulating machine sales, there are two aspects to consider: first, one could interpret this system as an effort of IBM to expand the tabulator monopoly to punch cards. Telser (1965), however, has the opinion that punch card usage is a measure of machine utilization, and thus, machine utility. Due to the freedom to charge a high mark-up on punch cards within a bundle, IBM succeeded in exploiting their customers utility according to the intensity of tabulating machine usage. This wouldn't have been possible without tying in card sales, since each customer paid the same price for the tabulating machines. Tie-in sales which are identical to pure bundling under the single unit purchase assumption, extract consumer surplus more effectively than single pricing which is not appropriate to quantify customers utility. A similar example is reported by Blackstone (1975), where Xerox only leased its copy machines to its customers and based prices on the number of processed copies. First after 1962, they additionally offered a sales option which, however, was so unattractive that most customers held on to the leasing option.

Most analytical studies considering optimal bundling strategies were conducted within the price discrimination tradition. The classic contribution of Adams and Yellen (1976) provides a benchmarking of each bundling strategy with respect to pure price discrimination which is known to be the most profitable form of pricing. They examine a two-product monopolist when the products are independent in demand for all consumers (discrete, additive reservation prices). They consider an additive variable cost structure and no fix costs associated with each commodity. In addition, they assume that a customer will either purchase one unit of a commodity, or won't purchase it at all (no marginal utility of a second unit). Adams and Yellen show, that each pricing strategy (unbundled sales, pure and mixed bundling) has its advantages and disadvantages in relation to the other two. The two major factors, determining the profitability of either form are the level of cost and the distribution of customers in the reservation price space. A strongly negative correlation of reservation prices, for instance, is shown to favor bundling strategies as opposed to single pricing. For a symmetric demand distribution and a relatively high cost level, a single pricing strategy may be preferred. In addition, Cready (1991) addresses profitability conditions for premium bundling. In case of overall positively correlated reservation prices and a strong negative correlation among consumers with relatively low reservation prices, premium bundling can be more profitable than unbundled sales, pure or mixed bundling. The major practical problem, of course, is how to prevent customers from buying the bundle components individually and then self-bundling. Although he mentions couponing and rebates as potential tools to employ premium bundling, realizations of this practice seem to be rare.

Dansby and Conrad (1984) dropped the assumption of additive reservation prices. They examine the case, where a bundle may either contain an unwanted component (value reducing) or provide additional value beyond the aggregated values of the individual items (value enhancing). They conclude that this diversity in consumers' bundle preferences can be an additional incentive for firms to bundle, even if the firm has no monopoly power. Schmalensee (1984) for the first time developed numerical criteria on which bundling strategy turns out to be more profitable. Thereby, he assumes that buyers reservation prices follow a bivariate normal distribution. Stating the profit function and the according extremal problem, he shows that there is no explicit representation of an optimal price. Thus, he obtains profitability conditions in either bundling case by numerical analysis. He expands the result of Adams and Yellen (1976) for pure bundling and shows that a negative correlation in consumers' reservation prices is no necessary condition for pure bundling being more profitable than unbundled sales. Actually, pure bundling is shown to be always more profitable, if reservation prices have a positive correlation and the cost level is low enough. Furthermore he shows that mixed bundling is not more profitable than pure bundling in the case of perfect positive correlation of reservation prices. As in the pure bundling case he suggests that mixed bundling is more profitable than unbundled sales, if the cost level is low enough, but he claims that his analysis of an optimal mixed bundling strategy is not complete.

Eppen, Hanson and Martin (1991) present seven strategic guidelines for the successful implementation of a bundling strategy which partly accrue from a qualitative interpretation of the Hanson/Martin model cited above. They particularly address the opportunity of bundling to expand demand ("aggregation bundling", "trade-up bundling" and "loyalty bundling"). Other strategic goals supported by bundling are expansion of monopoly power to competitive markets (Warhit, 1980; Palfrey, 1983) and increase of product enhancement and possibilities of product differentiation from competitors (Porter, 1985).

A number of recent studies address to the advantages of unbundling commodities in competitive markets which seems to become more popular over time (Jackson,

1985). Whereas Schmalensee (1982) states that a monopolist will never choose to bundle its indivisible goods with the goods of a perfectly competitive industry, if the goods are unrelated in production and consumption, Carbajo, De Meza and Seidman (1990) show that the monopolist may well bundle with the product of an imperfectly competitive industry. They explain their findings with the strategic role of bundling in the presence of imperfect competition as a mean to induce rivals to compete less aggressively. Considering industrial systems, Porter (1985) identifies two managerial decisions that system suppliers are facing. A system supplier may maintain its current strategy and try to strengthen its current market position by using advanced technology to offer customers higher system benefits. The second option is to unbundle complete systems and sell system components separately. This enables the supplier to possibly withdraw from the market for some system components and "outsource" these products. Wilson, Weiss and John (1990) provide some market conditions, which may favor unbundling, as potentially higher margins for unbundled systems which may stem from a reduced price elasticity of the single components. Besides demand expansion issues, they also mention increasing integration and modularity: this raises the risk of pure bundling strategies, because customers are able to obtain desired components by simply mixing and matching components from different suppliers. Guiltinan (1987) compares mixed bundling strategies and unbundled sales with complementary consumer services. He particularly stresses the necessity of clear strategic marketing objectives and a thorough analysis of the specific bundling program.

Other marketing investigations aim at the customers' perception of bundled products. It is well known (Gaeth et al., 1991) that in particular customers with a low information level are willing to pay a higher price for the bundle than the prices for the individual items would suggest. It is astonishing though and must be considered a bad sales practice that in car purchases, for instance, customers are induced to buy individual car options which are a subset of an offered package, at a higher price than they would be charged for the entire package. In this framework, Yadav and Monroe (1993) examine the transaction value of a bundle with a focus on customers perception of savings in a bundle price. They promote offering two small savings (on the purchase of all bundle items separately and on the bundle purchase) instead of offering only one large saving on the bundle. They stress however, that results seems to depend on the semantic format of the specific presentation method. Nagle (1987) generally suggests that bundled items at one price are more likely to induce a customer to purchase them, than separately offered and priced products.

In the preceding models only little insight was gained on the optimal composition of a bundle and the issue of optimal pricing. Most recent contributions consider general product line design in the context of conjoint analysis. Zufryden (1977,82) was the first to formulate a share-maximizing product line problem as an integer program, assuming deterministic preferences. He suggests to select the product line directly from idiosyncratic part worths data (for an exhaustive review of commercial applications of conjoint analysis see Cattin and Wittink (1989)). Kohli and Sukumar (1990) present a 0-1 integer formulation how to structure product lines maximizing share, buyer's utility and seller's profit. Since the particular problems are NP-hard, they also propose a dynamic programming heuristic which extends the result of Kohli and Krishnamurti (1987) for choosing a share maximizing single item. Other contributions by Green and Krieger (1985), and McBride and Zufryden (1988) consider a finite reference set of candidate items from which they select the product line. Dobson and Kalish (1988) measure consumer's utility in reservation prices and consumer's choice behavior by the obtained surplus. They explicitly consider fix and variable production costs and propose heuristics to solve the resulting non-linear problem to maximize profit. Hanson and Martin (1991) provide a practical method for a single firm how to bundle the products in its line and to find the optimal prices for the bundles. Their approach is based on the assumptions of a monopolist facing segmented customer demand with deterministic reservation price arrays for each segment. The underlying structure is sub-additive, and is therefore able to capture cost synergies arising, for instance, by reduced setup costs for a particular bundle in production. They state the single firm bundle pricing problem as a mixed linear integer program, where the number of constraints grows exponentially with the number of considered products (see 3.3). Due to the intractability of this method for a large number of considered potential bundles, they present an algorithm using a decomposition approach with only linear growth in the constraints of the master program. The algorithm was successfully tested with a number of generated test problems. In general, most deterministic mixed integer programs are flexible and can be well adapted to the institutional structure of the problem. On the other hand, this approach is frequently computationally intractable and objectives are non-concave.

Stochastic choice models mainly focus on consumer segmentation and utility measurement (Ogawa, 1987), whereas many contributions explored the aggregate utility structure as linear interaction (Green, 1984), quadratic (Louvière and Woodworth, 1983), logit (McFadden, 1974), probit (Daganzo, 1979), maximum score (Manski, 1975), or Generalized Extreme Value (McFadden, 1980). Particularly widespread is the multinomial logit model (McFadden, 1986) and has been applied by many authors to product line design and pricing (e.g. Kamakura and Russell, 1989; Allenby and Rossi, 1991). In a recent contribution, Hanson and Martin (1994) present an interesting approach how to optimize a non-concave profit function using the logit model. They point out that a lack of at least quasi-concavity of the objective may cause any solution method to terminate at a local optimum. To avoid this, they apply a path-following procedure (Garcia and Zangwill, 1981) which defines a homotopy between the original non-concave problem and a concave problem with a higher degree of randomness in consumer's choice behavior. Starting with the "easy" modified problem, they use the optimal price vector of a preceding step as a starting point for a subsequent less concave problem. Thus, they drag along a closed path with constant increment for the homotopy defining parameters and end up solving the original problem after a finite number of steps. Although this method does not guarantee to find the global optimum of a function, several optimization runs with different parameter sets increase confidence in the quality of the obtained result.

In the next section we will address the potential shortcomings of the presented literature from the viewpoint of an automobile manufacturer.

3.3   Option Bundling in the Automobile Industry

In this section we intend to characterize the bundling of car options within the framework developed in the last section. We will illuminate a couple of branch-specific properties which characterize the special structure and requirements of the problem. We will put a special emphasis on the potential implications of bundling to product complexity and deproliferation. Finally, we address to the opportunities of efficiently collecting the required data and implementing an analytical optimization process.

3.3.1   The Car Manufacturer's Perspective

For most car producers, the maximum profitability of their car lines is achieved in the first third of a car's life cycle. The second year of a car model is usually the most successful one: the learning curve in production decreases the manufacturing costs, sales volumes are high without spending a lot of money for sales incentives or other allowances, and warranty costs are still low (see Figure 3.3). After two years, production costs converge, variant driven complexity costs increase, and a lot of marketing expenses are necessary to prevent sales volumes from dropping rapidly. In this phase, operating profit frequently is not high enough to cover variable and fix costs. It is even possible to run into negative variable profit, where net sales can not even cover variable costs (a situation, where the production of the car should be terminated from an economic point of view, or at least no money should be spent to increase sales volumes). In addition, leanly equipped cars are sold with very low margins due to competitive pricing strategies.

In the domestic market, the largest fraction of the potential profit from car sales stems from the additional equipment which is sold along with the pure "transportation feature". In particular after the two years mentioned above, option profit is the vital source of most small and medium size car lines. Car producers who ex-

Figure 3.3: Profit Evolution During Lifecycle

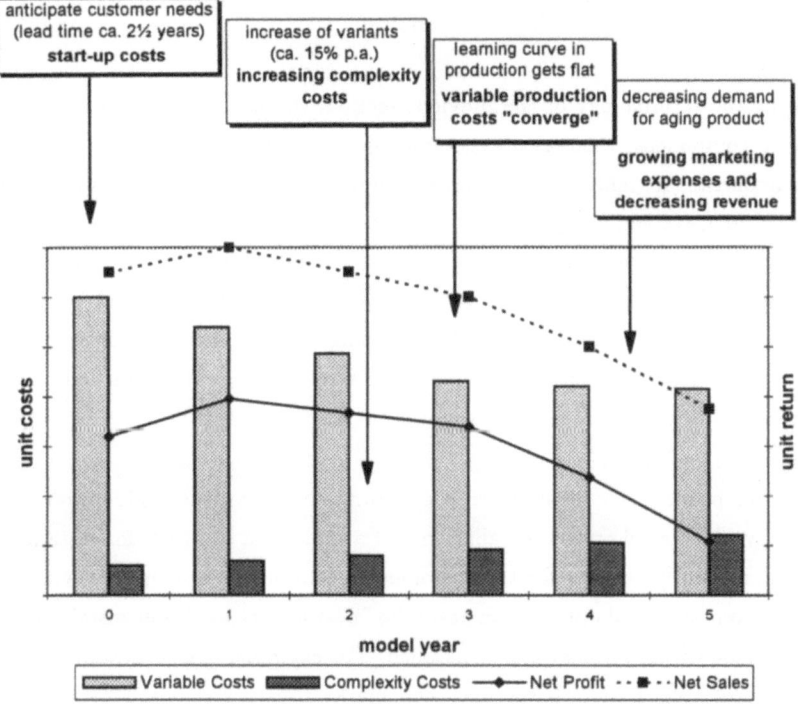

port their cars are facing long transportation lead times, and thus a very extended forecast horizon, frequently up to four months shipping time from Asia to Europe. In the destination country, large inventories and highly sophisticated distribution systems are not economic for only moderate sales volumes. Exclusively offering free-flow options is usually not sufficient to achieve profit targets on the domestic market and virtually infeasible for the exporting manufacturer from a distribution cost standpoint. Stochastic option bundling and bundle pricing provides a method to "tailor" equipment packages which optimally exploit the demand structure of a particular market. Furthermore, the risk-pooling effect of option packages decreases the finished goods inventory which is necessary to maintain a certain service level. Option packages utilize scale economies, if they are targeted for an aggregate market and thus reduce customer lead time through increased availability. It is also a matter of fact that option packages have a positive impact on quality, serviceability, resale value, and image of entire car brands. The impact of bundling to production costs will be assessed in the next section.

Using the terminology of the previous section, the basic car can be viewed as the tying component, whereas all customer specific options can be considered as tied components. Roughly speaking, these commodity options of a car could be separated in substitutive and complementary items, whereas we are not able to strictly assign each option to one of these two categories. The power door lock system clearly has complementary character, a 2.0 ltr., four cylinder engine is a substitutive commodity among an optional 2.5 ltr. or a 2.5 ltr. V6 engine for a particular car line. However, would a radio with cassette player and a radio with CD player be complementary or substitutive items?

For our purposes, it seems more adequate to choose another differentiation termi-nology. A delayed option installation – of a radio or a sun-roof, for instance – may be significantly cheaper for the customer than to order these options with the new car. Even electrical options can easily be "postponed" by dealer installation, if the necessary wiring harness is pre-installed. For example, due to a radio penetration of almost 95% across all car lines and markets, each dashboard harness contains the necessary radio connection wires. Car producers such as Hyundai Motors con-sciously overequip their wiring harnesses, since option postponement is crucial to run their business in the European market. However, a subsequent installation of a dual airbag system or central door locks affects too many car components and thus would mean tremendous additional costs for the customer. Therefore, a distinction between options that can be postponed and options which are tedious to physically separate from the basic car, seems to be obvious. This is supported by the observa-tion, that more and more car manufacturers make bundling of options as radio or trailer hitch a dealer's business to reduce the variance of build combinations in car production.

On the manufacturer side we observe three different option bundling approaches, in form of *trim level definitions, equipment packages* and *special editions.* Trim levels are the basic car equipment definitions, as the L, LS, GL or GLS version of a car type, obtained by successively adding on (door options, ABS, ...) or upgrading (engine size, radio,...) components. Mostly, the product program starts with a very leanly equipped car, and ends with the luxury version, providing a lot of standard equipment. A hierarchical structure of trim levels aims at, what Eppen, Hanson and Martin (1991) call "trade-up" bundling, where a customer is induced to purchase a higher graded trim level. However, many trim levels can also have a "trade-down" impact. The manufacturer's profit margins for the basic trim levels without additionally ordered options can range from low to almost zero, due to high dealer allowances. Option packages, however, are usually coupled to one or more trim levels, and consist of combinations of components which are not covered by the standard equipment. Sometimes, specific options are bundled to give the package a certain meaning, as heated seats and mirrors, fog lamps, special tires and exterior colors within a "cold weather" package. In general, seller allowances are lower for additional equipment, thus manufacturer's profit generated from selling a leanly equipped car plus a comfort package is higher than obtained by the sale of a lean GLS version, which already contains the comfort package as a standard. Special editions of a car line, as the Opel ASTRA California or the VW Golf GTI Edition, usually aim at an increase of production capacity utilization by stimulating demand. These car models are offered for a limited time at a price which often only allows for very low margins. We will propose our approach as a method to find the profit maximizing option packages for a given scenario of trim levels. Since this represents the most general case, strategies to find optimal trim levels or design a special edition vehicle can be easily derived.

We will consider a stochastic formulation of the problem to maximize profit by creating and pricing car option bundles (as opposed to dynamic programming or multi-period optimization) due to four major reasons:

- Consumer utilities for most options are highly variable; since we are dealing with a large number of options, a segmentation of customers according to their reservation prices (via cluster analysis, for instance) still results in reservation price distributions within each segment for a particular option with considerable standard deviations.

- Stochastic utility measurement also includes aspects of imperfect competition among several producers: the variability and the expected value of a consumer's reservation price for a product reflects the prices of competitive offers.

- Even knowing the particular utilities of each option or option bundle, choice behavior can only be mapped taking into account cannibalization effects, and thus the influence of the entire product line on the purchasing behavior. Thus, a deterministic 0-1 choice rule does not capture these effects. Using specially structured choice models, we can even incur game theoretic competition between trim levels or even entire car lines.

- The implementation cost of the presented approach will be minimal. This is of special interest, because probabilistic models in general are less sensitive to data perturbations than their deterministic counterparts.

The stochastic bundling model places very few restrictions on the underlying cost structure. We will consider variable costs of any type as well as fix costs associated with each option package. This takes into account proliferation and scale economies. We will also explicitly incur imperfect competition by imposing upper bounds on the optimized bundle prices. Switching from a higher trim level to a lower trim level (a trim level will be viewed as a segment) plus a package will be avoided by requiring lower bounds on the optimal prices which are high enough to make this form of trading down unattractive.

3.3.2   Bundling and Deproliferation

Proliferation avoidance has become one of the major targets of a new car program and primarily affects the main development functions, i.e. design, advance engineering, product development, prototyping and manufacturing engineering. Provided a timely and comprehensive product development, the start of production concept has reduced build combinations to a minimum number, which still assures the intended market performance. However, with the increasing number of platforms and car lines, substantial forces are driving proliferation. As a result, development costs

may even double from a new car model to its predecessor. Figure 3.4 shows that
the number of system variants increases by almost 60 % in the first four years of a
car's life cycle.

Figure 3.4: System Variant Explosion

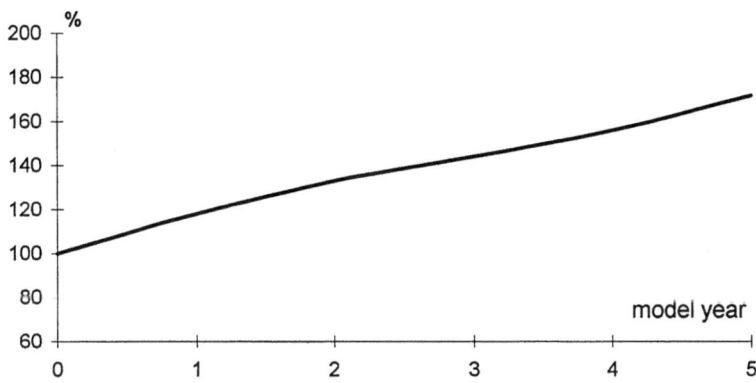

This mainly happens due to three reasons:

- After start of production of a new car, sharp proliferation targets are missing. Expected total life cycle programs do not contain objectives for addition/deletion of build combinations considering the impact at the systems level.

- Often, there are no means to track the car program's complexity state. Changing demands of both legal and marketing requirements affect the justification and profitability of build combinations and system variants. If an adequate monitoring tool is missing, decisions upon replacement or deletion of existing variants are difficult, if not impossible.

- The total cost chain is not transparent. A product engineer's proposal to add a new part number to the system is a pure tradeoff between technical requirements and variable product/manufacturing costs. Marketing establishes product changes with a strong focus on market acceptance. Very seldom, these decisions are additionally based upon complexity costs.

Build combinations reflect the complexity of the final product as it is offered on the market. They also drive savings in distribution and assembly. Reducing the number of build combinations strongly impacts the product system level at which deproliferation savings are determined for the main cost blocks development, manufacturing and purchasing. Major cost savings can be expected for

- Engines/Transmissions

- Body-In-White

- Chassis

- Doors

- Exhaust systems

- Electric/electronic.

Figure 3.5: Proliferation Drivers Exhaust System

Complexity Driver	Manifold	Support Transm.	Decoupling	Catalytic Converter	Center Mufler	Rear Mufler
Engine Type	•	•	•	•	•	•
Emission Norm	•	-	-	•	•	-
Noise Standard	-	•	•	-	-	-
Underbody	•	-	-	•	•	•
Transmission	•	•	•	•	•	-
Supplier	-	-	-	•	-	•
Special Vehicle	•	-	-	•	•	•

For most of the above mentioned product systems, proliferation is option driven and in turn has an impact on other systems. The dash-panel as a subsystem of the body-in-white for instance has different shapes and layouts depending on options as transmission style, steering mechanism, air conditioning and airbag. The exhaust system consists of its major components front pipe, transmission support, decoupling elements, catalytic converter, center muffler and rear muffler plus additional heat shields. Figure 3.5 shows the key proliferation drivers for the exhaust system. Again, engine/transmission combinations, trim levels and several free-flow options influence the number of exhaust system variations. Bundling certain body styles, engines and transmissions, by commonsense Pareto analyses, the number of exhaust system variants can frequently be reduced by more than 50%.

Many deproliferation activities, such as modified technical solutions, modularity concepts and sourcing methods, aim at the system variant complexity and not at primarily limiting the number of build combinations. Pure option bundling however presents an opportunity to already decrease the number of build combinations by magnitudes.

There are some car producers who still defend the business strategy to build "everything for everybody". Deleting free-flow options and offering them exclusively within packages is rejected due to the potential loss of sales and the lack of knowledge of the total cost chain. In particular for non-activity based costing systems, the offset between additional variable costs and deproliferation cost savings does not justify a deletion of variants. The major trend, however, is to offer a new car with a very limited number of engine-transmission combinations, body styles and free-flow options, together with a set of equipment packages. In the next section, we analyze the common sales tendencies of several car manufacturers by means of product program and sales volume.

3.3.3 Sales Strategy Benchmarking

In this section we want to clarify the question, how the attractivity of a car is influenced by the variety of build combinations offered to the customer. For this purpose we have selected 15 vehicles of different brands which are competing in the German middle-class market segment and are comparable in engine power, engine size and price. All cars are either 4-door sedans or 5-door limousines with 4 cylinder engines. Each car type may be available as sedan and limousine in several trim levels. All utilized data stem from official customer brochures, which were available between July and October 1993. To benchmark the different sales practices, we have chosen 23 options from three ranges:

<u>Technical Features:</u> Anti-Lock Brake System (ABS), driver/passenger airbag, air conditioning, burglar alarm, check control (visual control of most electronical car functions), cruise control, electronic differential lock (rear wheel drive), respectively electronic traction control (front wheel drive), immobilizer (new anti-theft device), power door lock, power steering, automatic transmission.

<u>Interior Equipment:</u> Audio systems (incl. radio/CD, antenna, speaker diversity), electric sun blind rear, headrests rear, multi function display, power windows front, seats (incl. adjustment, heating, support), tachometer, tilt steering.

<u>Exterior Equipment:</u> Heat absorbing screens, integrated fog lamps, power mirror, sunroof (electric, manual, glass).

It is clear that a feature like "seats" may consist of several options as height adjustment, heated seats or sport seats. Except "audio systems" we do not consider options which can be easily postponed, since many customer brochures do not completely reflect this supply. We neither incur options like exterior colors and upholstery which are undergoing relatively fast product changes.

Figure 3.6 shows for each considered car model its number of body and trim styles, engine power and displacement, as well as price range (incl. 15% VAT). Furthermore, we show the new car registrations in Germany from January to May 1994. The total number of build components was generated by counting the combinatorial variants of each car type/body style/trim level with respect to the 23 sample options, considering all restrictions that may apply. Finally, we have counted the number of sample options which are standard equipment and which can not be ordered with the car model with medium trim level. It can be observed that the variety of offered car combinations ranges from four (Hyundai) to more than 29 million (Mercedes Benz). Some producers only offer one body style and trim level (Audi, Hyundai, MB), others many more (Ford, Mazda, Opel). The market leader of this particular segment is the Mercedes Benz C 180, followed by the BMW 316i, the Ford Mondeo 1.8, the Opel

Figure 3.6: Benchmarking of Customer Specific Supply

Car	models	hp	displ.(ltrs.)	sales price (DM)	build combos
Audi A4	1	100	1.595	36,000	2,064,384
BMW 316	2	102	1.596	36,500-39,000	5,398,528
Citroen Xantia	2	121	1.998	37,000-40,500	1,200
Fiat Croma	3	115	1.995	34,900-42,500	52
Ford Mondeo	6	115	1.796	33,910-40,300	33,024
Hyundai Sonata	1	139	1.997	33,790	4
MB C 180	1	122	1.799	40,825	29,196,288
Mazda 626	5	115	1.991	34,450-36,950	28
Nissan Primera	2	115	1.998	33,595-34,495	96
Opel Vectra 2.0	8	115	1.998	33,605-38,515	365,056
Peugeot 405	2	101	1.762	32,930-34,690	448
Renault Laguna	2	113	1.998	34,400-36,900	208
Toyota Carina	4	107	1.587	28,800-33,620	32
Volvo 460	1	109	1.998	32,500	1,024
VW Passat	3	115	1.984	36,900-43,860	850,518

Vectra 2.0 and the Toyota Carina 1.6. An interesting question is, whether there can be found common patterns among the different car brands. For this purpose, we have calculated an average price for each option and subtracted it from the original price of each car which contains the particular option as a standard. The resulting "neutral" price can be viewed as a baseline price for pure transportation service plus upgrade possibilities. In Figure 3.7 we have plotted the number of offered option combinations in a logarithmic scaling as a function of neutral price. The different manufacturers can easily be assigned to clusters which reflect where the particular car was built. The Asian producers offer a drastically reduced car variety at a low price, with South Korean Hyundai as an extreme. The European producers except for German producers offer a rather uniform number of variants, however with price differences of almost 5,000 DM. It is remarkable that Peugeot and Citroen differ a lot in price, although both are belonging to the PSA group. Peugeot has put a lot of effort in its deproliferation activities recently and has passed its cost advantage to the

Figure 3.7: Passenger Car Equipment Strategies

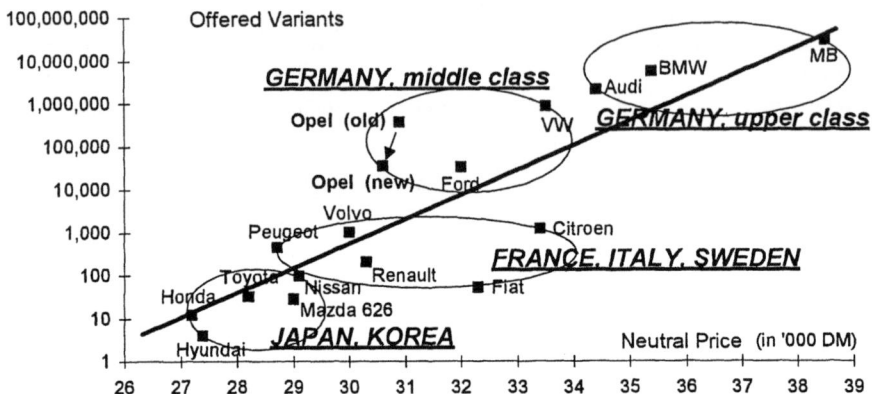

customer in form of relatively low prices. The German manufacturer cluster shows the largest number of variations and the highest neutral prices. Ford has reduced its offered combinations essentially by option packages and hierarchical trim levels, while maintaining a moderate price level. Opel is "cheapest in cluster", however with too many offered variants. VW, Audi (belongs to the VW group) and BMW are close to each other with many variants and high prices. The MB C 180 was the first successful try of Mercedes Benz to buy in the medium segment and is the most expensive car of all.

Furthermore, we have drawn a trend line for the price and variant data in Figure 3.7. The trend suggests that there is a certain relationship between the two variables, and eventually the customer is paying for the dubious freedom to select his individual car. Roughly speaking, there are three statistical outliers: the old Opel Vectra, the Citroen Xantia and the Fiat Croma. Opel, above the regression line, offered too many variants at a too low price, and thus tried to reduce their offered combinations at almost unchanged prices. Fiat and Citroen present themselves with reduced offer of combinations at elevated prices.

Of course, we can not claim to fully explain the mechanisms of price, variety of offered combinations and customer response, since we have only illuminated a small subset of all important parameters. In spite of its high prices, the MB C 180 has the highest sales volume of the current year in class which could be explained by its outstanding quality and image. However, the presented conclusions for the German middle class car market can essentially be extended to other European markets or even the Japanese market (where Asian and European manufacturers switch roles), as well as to the small and – somewhat restricted – upper class car segment.

To increase the explanatory value of Figure 3.7 and include "soft" decision criteria, such as company image, perceived quality, and so forth, more empirical data has to be collected to carry out a multivariable regression analysis.

3.3.4 Practical Implementation of the Bundle Optimization

To fully profit from simultaneously obtaining product definition, deproliferation and pricing decisions from a single tool, we also need to take into account some practical questions. The answers to these questions will serve as a kind of guideline when we attack the theoretical problem.

How can one collect, update and check the required data and what does it cost? Data collection problems are one major reason, why many important pricing decisions must be performed with too little information and why many analytical decision tools can not be properly applied. From Figure 3.8 we can see that the key data for an optimization consists of the utility/demand structure and the total cost structure, including fix and variable costs.

With respect to the demand data we will use the disaggregated forecast data, already considered in chapter 2. The common way to elicit consumer's preferences and reservation prices is to perform so-called car clinics, where a number of potential customers are confronted with several car types, representing an incomplete factorial design for a subsequent conjoint analysis. Each presented car is equipped with a combination of options which are to be assessed, and ranked by the consumers among other shown cars. Since it is only possible to present a very small fraction of all option combinations as "hardware" (usually less than 20 cars), the demand structure obtained by a subsequent multivariate regression is highly sensitive to changes of the test design. Thus, the explanatory value of the car clinic data is questionable.

Figure 3.8: Option Bundling Information Flow

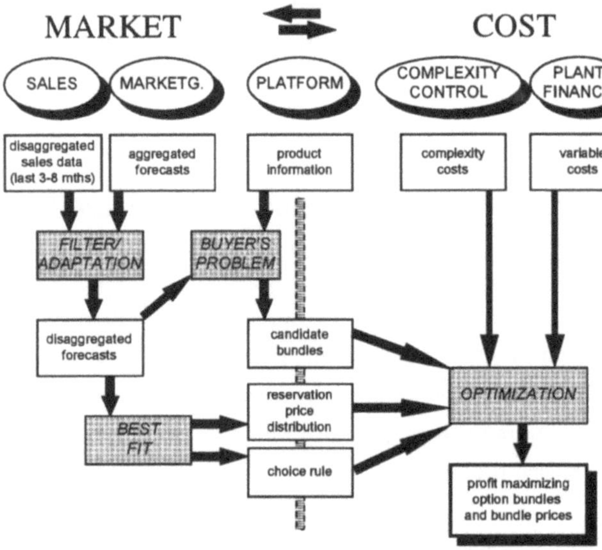

Furthermore, frequently occurring sample and answer biases, in combination with the high costs have caused a lot of criticism of the validity and feasibility of this method. Since our disaggregated forecast data reflects actual purchase behavior and is consistent with product program and option forecasts, we will use this strategic database information as a "simulated survey" (see Curry, 1993). However, we stress again the fact that this data base does not include loss-of-goodwill data which can only be evaluated empirically. Hence, there will be no extra cost to investigate the demand structure, and we avoid any source of error due to misinterpreted "sales" data. In section 3.3.2 we will show how to use disaggregated car data to obtain part-worths data for each option using conjoint analysis. The candidate bundles considered in the price finding stage will be obtained by a 0-1 integer programming approach. We will even be able to estimate reservation price distributions for arbitrary customer segments and bundles by interpolating truncated price information by a composite normal distribution.

The required information on variable production costs is twofold: we need to consider product costs of the control devices for each option (as a central airbag sensor and inflating system), as well as direct and indirect labor costs, related to the assembly or installation of each option in the car. A good first approximation of the "real" variable and fix cost structure is to use the wiring harness cost data. Most synergy effects of option packages are due to less material or shorter labor times for the harness installation. Process costs of the harness assembly are seldom explicitly known, but frequently estimated by planning or cost tracking departments evaluating labor time effort. Data consistency and update is assured best, if the data is stored in a centralized database, which is owned and administered by the responsible department with a read-only access for all data processing company sections. Although this sounds like a matter of course – the acceptance of any computer-based strategy development prevalently depends on the validity of the input data. Thus, it is desirable to base the bundle optimization on an aggregate level on the same forecast data as is used for a business plan, the cost structure should be identical to the data used for financial analyses of a product program.

Another question that sets the frame for the optimization is the question, who the potential user of such an optimization tool is. Since product definition and pricing decisions have to be made simultaneously to maximize profit, the suggested procedure has to be performed jointly by the particular car platform management and the finance departments. Since a car line is often subject to conceptual changes during a production cycle (so-called running changes), or forecast errors decrease due to a shortened forecast horizon, an optimization may be necessary periodically. Hence, side constraints and the demand/cost structure may change at an "elementary" level which makes an involvement of computation specialists indispensable. Nevertheless, to maintain flexibility and build up acceptance, the general optimization procedure should finally be available as a user-friendly local (PC or workstation based) decision tool.

To judge the validity and quality of prediction of our model, historical car, cost and demand data can be used. In section 3.4 we will analyze a real large-scale sample problem to test our method.

3.4   Bundle Profit Maximization Under Uncertainty

In this section we will present an algorithm for the stochastic bundling problem. In section 3.4.1 we will define the subsequently used terminology and notation. The stochastic bundling model will be introduced in section 3.4.2 as a non-linear mixed-integer program. The concavity properties of our objective function mainly depend on the degree of randomness of our choice rule which will approximate purchase behavior in our model. As we will empirically demonstrate, the modeled demand structures frequently produce concave objective functions. In case of choice rules with low degree of randomness, the objective function will be non-concave and standard non-linear search procedures may get stuck in a poor local optimum. For this case we develop a heuristic algorithm following the path-following approach of Hanson and Martin (1994) and define a class of similar problems for the original problem. A homotopy will continuously transform a well-behaved concave problem into our original non-concave problem. Extremal properties of the well-behaved problem show only "small" changes, as we follow the homotope path towards the original problem. Thus, having found the global optimum for one profit function of our homotopy class, we show in section 3.4.3 that for small steps along the homotope path the global optimum of the resulting slightly modified profit function can be found in a neighborhood of the preceding optimum. In section 3.4.4 we will show how the required input data can be obtained, i.e., the generation of candidate bundles utilizing conjoint analysis and linear programming as well as "fitting" demand/reservation price distributions through interpolation of actual sales behavior by a Normal distribution. In section 3.4.5, we develop a decomposition solution algorithm, embedding the non-linear pricing sub-problem in a greedy-interchange heuristic (compare also chapter 2).

3.4.1 Notation and Terminology

At first we give a list of all parameters and variables used in the next sections:

Demand related parameters

r = the number of options considered.

k = $1, \ldots, r$.

m = the number of candidate option bundles.

m^* = the number of competitive option bundle offerings.

m_0 = maximum number of allowed bundles.

j = $1, \ldots, m$.

n = the number of customer segments.

i = $1, \ldots, n$.

N_i = number of customers in segment i.

u_j = upper bound for price of option bundle j.

w_{ki} = normalized part worth of option k for segment i.

Production related parameters

q = the number of constraints due to product restrictions.

t = $1, \ldots, q$.

s_{kt} = constraint coefficient of option k in restriction t.

b_t = right hand side of the production inequality constraints.

c_{ij} = variable cost of supplying one customer of segment i with option bundle j.

f_j = fix cost associated with option bundle j.

Stochastic parameters

U_{ij} = utility of customer segment i for bundle j.

α_i = choice parameter for segment i.

α = $(\alpha_1, \ldots, \alpha_n)$.

μ_{ij} = mean reservation price of segment i for bundle j.

σ_{ij} = standard deviation of reservation price.

ψ_{ij} = reservation price density function.

Ω_{ij} = domain of ψ_{ij}.

Ψ_{ij} = reservation price distribution function.

Decision variables

p_j = the price of bundle j.

y_j = $\begin{cases} 1 & \text{if bundle } j \text{ is produced} \\ 0 & \text{otherwise} \end{cases}$.

a_{kj} = $\begin{cases} 1 & \text{if option } k \text{ is contained in bundle } j \\ 0 & \text{otherwise} \end{cases}$.

Auxiliary variables

p = $(p_1, \ldots, p_m)$.

u = $(u_1, \ldots, u_m)$.

y = $(y_1, \ldots, y_m)$.

ς_{ij} = consumer surplus of segment i for bundle j.

π_{ij} = purchase probability of segment i for bundle j.

Π_i = probabilistic variable profit obtained by segment i.

Π = $\Pi_1 \cdot N_1 + \ldots + \Pi_n \cdot N_n$.

A_j = $\{a_{1j}, \ldots, a_{rj}\}$ (bundle j).

A = Mat $(a_{kj})_{k,j}$.

We consider $m \geq r + m_0$ candidate option bundles, for which we have to decide on m_0 bundles to be produced and what their price should be. Since we want to incur all options in our decision process and consider different bundling strategies, we define bundles $A_1, \ldots, A_r$ as "mandatory bundles" in form of the single options $(100 \ldots 00), \ldots, (000 \ldots 01)$. It is reasonable to limit the number of offered equipment bundles to retain clarity of offer for customers and sales-people. We consider n customer segments which can be viewed as the collection of customers of a particular trim level, for instance. Furthermore, we will take into account m^* competitive offers which are not under control of another car manufacturer. These competing bundles provide an alternative purchase option for each customer segment. Therefore, a customer of segment i, purchasing neither of the bundles $1 \ldots m$ is a brand switcher who is facing too high prices across our option bundle/base car offers.

The variable costs c_{ij} mainly consist of the material costs for bundle j for segment i plus assembly process costs. Assembly process data is usually stored in databases for all car lines and plants and updated periodically. One sequential record of such a database consists of a logical application restriction, which uniquely determines the bundle in process. In addition, it contains all processed part numbers, a description of the job and its duration, as well as general information on car type, plant and department. Thus, knowing the regional multipliers for labor time, we can aggregate all cost data for each particular bundle. As already mentioned earlier, fix costs f_j for bundle j are difficult to obtain. Similar to the wiring harnesses we charge each used part number with an estimated annual overhead, originating from holding stock, transportation, opportunity costs, and so forth.

We will impose upper bounds u_j for the price of bundle j because we may actively want to underprice a competing car model or a competitive option package. We assume $u_j > c_{ij}$ without loss for all $i \leq n$, otherwise we would produce bundle j with negative variable profit for at least one customer segment which we do not permit.

Matrix $\mathbf{A} \in \{0,1\}^{r \times m}$ is the component or attribute matrix and consists of all rows (bundles) A_j. At least we need to know how to price all single items, if we offer them. Hence, we will initialize X_t $(t \leq r)$ as the "bundles", consisting of the single option k. In the traditional economic literature, customer choice among different items of a product line is explained by the utility concept: a customer will choose the item which maximizes his or her utility. We will use this approach to explain purchase decisions for our bundles as well.

For each pair (i,j) let (Ω_{ij}, Ψ_{ij}) denote a probability space, where Ω_{ij} is the set of possible realizations of the uncertain parameter ω_{ij} and Ψ_{ij} the corresponding cumulative probability distribution. We will consider each bundle as a particular product with a composite, univariate density function. Since we want to allow for negative reservation prices for strong dislikes, we let $\Omega_{ij} = (-\infty, \infty)$, independently of i and j. We will generally suppose, that ω_{ij} is a continuous random variable, i.e.

$$\Psi_{ij}(p) = 1 - \int_{-\infty}^{p} \psi_{ij}(p')\, dp' \quad , \tag{3.1}$$

for all $p \in \Omega_{ij}$ and pairs (i,j). Hence, we define

$$\mu_{ij} = \int_{-\infty}^{\infty} p'\, \psi_{ij}(p')\, dp' \quad , \quad \sigma_{ij}^2 = \int_{-\infty}^{\infty} p'^2\, \psi_{ij}(p')\, dp' \tag{3.2}$$

as the mean, respectively standard deviation of the reservation price, if the integrals converge absolutely. The consumer surplus obtained by segment i purchasing bundle j $(i = 1, \ldots, m)$ is thus identical to the linear loss function

$$\varsigma_{ij}(p_j) = \int_{p_j}^{\infty} (p' - p_j)\, \psi_{ij}(p')\, dp' \quad , \tag{3.3}$$

with first and second order derivatives

$$\varsigma_{ij}'(p_j) = -\Psi_{ij}(p_j) \quad , \tag{3.4}$$

$$\varsigma_{ij}''(p_j) = \psi_{ij}(p_j) \quad . \tag{3.5}$$

For customer segment i, ς_{ij} with $m + 1 \leq j \leq m + m^*$ denotes the surpluses obtained by purchasing a competitive product. We assume no explicit dependency on the current bundle price vector $\mathbf{p}$.

$\pi_{ij}(\mathbf{A}, \mathbf{p})$ is the share of utility of segment i for bundle j. It expresses the probability, that customer segment i will choose bundle j among all bundles which result in a positive surplus for him. Several approaches exist how to define a share-of-utility rule. In the classic random utility framework under the assumption of independent and identically distributed extreme values for the stochastic components of segment i's utility for a bundle j, this probability can be written as the multinomial LOGIT function

$$\frac{\exp(U_{ij})}{\sum_{j=m+1}^{m+m^*} \exp(U_{ij}) + \sum_{j=1}^{m} \exp(U_{ij})} \tag{3.6}$$

(see Gumbel, 1958). However, since we want our model to adapt to different consumer profiles in terms of choice randomness, we prefer to apply a slightly more general approach. For fixed values of y_j and $\alpha_i \in [0, \infty)$ (compare Green and Krieger, 1992), we define the alpha choice rule by

$$\pi_{ij}(\mathbf{A}, \mathbf{p}, \mathbf{y}, \alpha_i) = \frac{U_{ij}^{\alpha_i} \cdot y_j}{\sum_{j=m+1}^{m+m^*} U_{ij}^{\alpha_i} + \sum_{j=1}^{m} U_{ij}^{\alpha_i} \cdot y_j} \quad . \tag{3.7}$$

Thus, the probability that segment i will choose bundle j among all other bundles is mainly determined by the ratio of the utility for bundle j and the sum of utility for all bundles, including competitor offers. The α_i's represent a segment specific exponential weight for the utilities. As we will see, α_i will serve as a measure of choice randomness.

The freedom to choose α_i allows this rule to closely match a given consumer choice behavior (see section 3.3.4). Furthermore, the alpha choice rule is comprising, or at least mimicking, several traditional choice rules. Assume that $y_j = 1$ without loss of generality. Obviously, $\pi_{ij}(\mathbf{A}, \mathbf{p}, \mathbf{y}, 0) = (m + m^*)^{-1}$, independent of $\mathbf{A}$ and $\mathbf{p}$, and thus represents the random choice behavior. On the other hand, $\pi_{ij}(\mathbf{A}, \mathbf{p}, \mathbf{y}, \infty) := \lim_{\alpha_i \to \infty} \pi_{ij}(\mathbf{A}, \mathbf{p}, y, \alpha_i)$ stands for the maximum utility choice rule, with

$$\pi_{ij}(\mathbf{A}, \mathbf{p}, \mathbf{y}, \infty) = \begin{cases} 1 & \text{if } U_{ij} = \max\{U_{i1}, \ldots, U_{i,m+m^*}\} \\ 0 & \text{otherwise} \end{cases} \quad . \tag{3.8}$$

For $\alpha = 1$, the model is equivalent to the Bradley-Terry-Luce rule. In general, the larger the α_i's will be, the more likely is it that segment i will choose the bundle which maximizes utility. The smaller α_i, the more random and thus more robust will choice behavior be with respect to product concept changes.

To obtain a computationally tractable measure, we define the utility for customer segment i by

$$U_{ij} = \varsigma_{ij}(p_j) \tag{3.9}$$

as the aggregated surplus of purchasing bundle j at a price p_j, where we assume that utility is completely explained by surplus.

Since we want to consider fix costs in our optimization, the choice probability depends on the decision on the y_j's., if in a certain optimization stage y_j switches from 0 to 1, for instance, π_{ij} takes a value greater than zero and choices of customer segments are redistributed according to the new surplus ratios. Vice versa, if

$y_j = 0$, bundle X_j has to be totally ignored from a share-of-utility rule. In the alpha rule, we put more and more emphasis on the bundle j which maximizes surplus for segment i among all bundles, as α_i increases. In Figure 3.9, we illustrate the behavior of $\pi_{ij}(\mathbf{A}, \mathbf{p}, \mathbf{y}, \alpha_i)$ for $n = 1$, $m = 3$, $m^* = 1$, $y = (1, \ldots, 1)$, and surpluses $(\varsigma_{11}, \ldots, \varsigma_{14}) = (5, 7, 9, 6)$.

Figure 3.9: Alpha Choice Rule

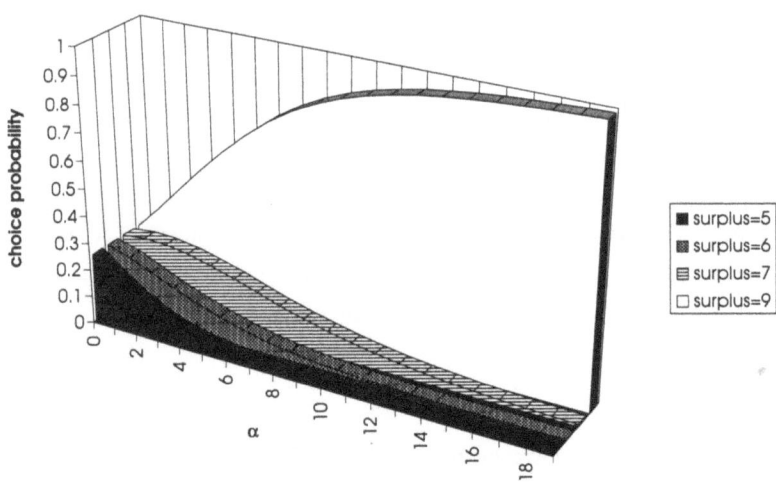

In the next section, we present and analyze the model which tells us how to compose a pool of candidate bundles, how to decide upon whether a particular bundle should be produced and how to price it.

3.4.2   Model Formulation and Analysis

The general problem to determine the composition of a product line and then to decide which products to produce and how to price them is usually decomposed in a *buyer's problem* and a *seller's problem* (see Kohli and Sukumar, 1988, among others). In the buyer's problem, we want to define bundles which, at a fixed price level, yield a high utility among the consumers. There are two general solution approaches: Delphi methods and mathematical methods. A Delphi session is an expert meeting, where decisions are achieved by discussion of opinions and facts, mainly based on experience and highly aggregated data. Despite the obvious doubts related to this subjective approach, Delphi methods are very common in automobile industry to even obtain pricing decisions. Here, we present a mathematical approach, representing the consumer's utility for a bundle by its part worth. The part worths are obtained by a hybrid conjoint analysis and will further on be used to solve the buyers problem.

Our conjoint analysis makes use of the disaggregated car data, which combines aggregated option forecasts and consumer's actual purchase behavior. We can interpret the data as a horse-race style design, where each consumer makes one choice among all possible car configurations. Each attribute (option) has exactly two levels 0 and 1. The resulting part worths for each option are normalized, such that $|w_{ki}| \leq 1$. Since conjoint analysis has become a standard tool, we will not discuss the data analysis in detail.

Due to product definitions and infeasible combinations, we need to translate all logical application restrictions (LAR) which apply to the considered options, into constraints for the optimization. Collecting and simplifying all resulting q inequalities, we get the matrix of production constraints S and the corresponding right hand side vector $(b_1, \ldots, b_q)$. Now we can formulate the buyer's problem:

Objective

$$\max \quad \sum_{k=1}^{r} \sum_{i=1}^{n} \sum_{j=1}^{m} w_{ki} a_{kj} \tag{3.10}$$

subject to

$$\sum_{k=1}^{r} \sum_{j=1}^{m} s_{kt} \cdot a_{kj} \leq b_t \quad t = 1, \ldots, q \quad , \tag{3.11}$$

$$a_{kj} \in \{0, 1\} \quad k = 1, \ldots, r, \ j = 1, \ldots, m \quad . \tag{3.12}$$

The objective function (3.10) takes into account the two levels of each attribute, where corresponding part worths just differ in their signs ($w_{ti} \rightarrow a_{kj} = 1$ and $-w_{ki} \rightarrow a_{kj} = 0$). Constraint (3.11) expresses the feasibility of each bundle from a product definition standpoint, constraint (3.12) requires a_{kj} to be a 0-1 variable.

The integer program above is relatively easy to solve since all production restrictions for one option can usually be coded with five to ten inequalities. The program can even be relaxed to a linear program with constraints $a_{kj} \geq 0$ and $a_{kj} \leq 1$ replacing constraint (3.12), since the solutions will turn out to almost exclusively take values close to 0 or 1.

The remaining problems, how to analytically elicit reservation price distributions from demand data and how to determine the "best fit" for the choice parameter α will be solved in section 3.4.4. For ease of notation we define the profit contribution of one customer in segment i

$$\Pi_i(\mathbf{A}, \mathbf{p}, \mathbf{y}, \alpha_i) := \sum_{j=1}^{m} (p_j - c_{ij}) \, \pi_{ij}(\mathbf{A}, \mathbf{p}, \mathbf{y}, \alpha_i) \, \Psi_{ij}(p_j) \quad , \tag{3.13}$$

and the overall profit

$$\Pi(X, p, y, \alpha) := \sum_{i=1}^{n} N_i \, \Pi_i(X, p, y, \alpha_i) \quad . \tag{3.14}$$

The function Π_i can be interpreted as follows: if there is only one bundle offered at a price p_1, the purchase probability for a customer from segment i is $\Psi_{i1}(p_1)$. This probability is reduced by the factor π_{ij}, if several bundles are offered and the customer has to choose the one, which maximizes his personal surplus. Now we can state the central stochastic bundle pricing problem (SBP):

Objective

$$\max \quad -\sum_{j=1}^{m} f_j y_j \, + \, \Pi(\mathbf{A}, \mathbf{p}, \mathbf{y}, \alpha) \quad , \tag{3.15}$$

subject to

$$\sum_{j=r+1}^{m} y_j \leq m_0 \quad , \tag{3.16}$$

$$0 \leq p_j \leq u_j \quad j = 1, \ldots, m \quad , \tag{3.17}$$

$$y_j \in \{0, 1\} \quad j = 1, \ldots, m \quad . \tag{3.18}$$

Additionally, we either have the pure bundling constraints

$$a_{kj} \cdot (y_k + y_j) \leq 1 \quad k = 1, \ldots, r, \; j = r+1, \ldots, m \quad , \tag{3.19}$$

$$\sum_{j=1}^{m} a_{kj} y_k \geq 1 \quad k = 1, \ldots, r \quad , \tag{3.20}$$

or the mixed bundling constraint

$$y_j = 1 \quad j = 1, \ldots, r \quad . \tag{3.21}$$

In the profit function (3.15), we consider fix costs for each bundle under pricing control and variable costs for each bundle and segment. Competitive bundles are assumed to have cost and price 0, and hence do not appear explicitly under the second sum. However, their surplus contribution is still contained in $\pi_{ij}(\mathbf{A}, \mathbf{p}, \mathbf{y}, \alpha_i)$ and enforces that

$$\sum_{j=1}^{m} \pi_{ij}(\mathbf{A}, \mathbf{p}, \mathbf{y}, \alpha_i) < 1 \quad \forall i \leq n \tag{3.22}$$

for $m^* \geq 1$. Inequality (3.16) allows only for at most m_0 bundles to be produced. The range for the optimal price is bounded as a reaction to competition with other manufacturers in constraint (3.17). In constraint (3.18) we state the 0-1 constraint for y_j. We can do without any choice constraints, because consumer's choice behavior is entirely explained by the alpha rule.

Furthermore, we want to distinguish between pure and mixed bundling strategies. In the pure bundling case, constraint (3.19) enforces that no single option is produced which is already contained in a bundle, and (3.20) guarantees that all options are actually offered. The mixed bundling case is less complicated: in (3.21) we just require all single options to be produced.

We should remark that the presented model is conservative in the sense that for each segment the sum of choice probabilities for all bundles is always less or equal to one. Hence, we assume that each customer will at most purchase only one bundle.

To investigate the extremal behavior of the non-linear objective function $\Pi(\mathbf{A}, \mathbf{p}, \mathbf{y}, \alpha)$ in (3.15) and the implementation of a direction finding solution method (see 3.4.3), we are interested in the partial derivatives of the profit function with respect to price p_l:

$$\frac{\partial \Pi_i(\mathbf{A}, \mathbf{p}, \mathbf{y}, \alpha_i)}{\partial p_l} = \pi_{il}(\mathbf{A}, \mathbf{p}, \mathbf{y}, \alpha_i)\left(\Psi_{il}(p_l) - (p_l - c_{il})\psi_{il}(p_l)\right)$$

$$+ \sum_{j=1}^{m}(p_j - c_{ij}) \cdot \frac{\partial \pi_{ij}(\mathbf{A}, \mathbf{p}, \mathbf{y}, \alpha_i)}{\partial p_l} \cdot \Psi_{ij}(p_j) \quad . \tag{3.23}$$

Let's assume without loss of generality that, if we want to differentiate a function with respect to p_j, the corresponding y_j is equal to 1. We need to know the partial derivatives of the alpha rule function $\pi_{ij} := \pi_{ij}(X, p, y, \alpha_i)$ with respect to p_j and p_l:

$$\frac{\partial \pi_{ij}}{\partial p_j} = \alpha_i \cdot \frac{\Psi_{ij}(p_j)}{\varsigma_{ij}(p_j)} \cdot \pi_{ij}(\pi_{ij} - 1) < 0 \quad , \tag{3.24}$$

$$\frac{\partial \pi_{ij}}{\partial p_l} = \alpha_i \cdot \frac{\Psi_{il}(p_l)}{\varsigma_{il}(p_l)} \cdot \pi_{ij} \pi_{il} > 0 \quad . \tag{3.25}$$

$$\tag{3.26}$$

Thus, we obtain

$$
\begin{aligned}
\frac{\partial \Pi_i}{\partial p_j} &= \pi_{ij} \left[\Psi_{ij}(p_j) - (p_j - c_{ij}) \, \psi_{ij}(p_j) \right] \\
&+ \alpha_i \pi_{ij}(p_j) \cdot \frac{\Psi_{ij}(p_j)}{\varsigma_{ij}(p_j)} \cdot (\Pi_i - (p_j - c_{ij}) \Psi_{ij}(p_j)) \quad ,
\end{aligned}
\tag{3.27}
$$

and the partial derivative of the profit function Π is

$$\frac{\partial \Pi(\mathbf{A}, \mathbf{p}, \mathbf{y}, \alpha)}{\partial p_j} = \sum_{i=1}^{n} N_i \cdot \frac{\partial \Pi_i(\mathbf{A}, \mathbf{p}, \mathbf{y}, \alpha_i)}{\partial p_j} \quad . \tag{3.28}$$

Now we take the second partial of $\partial \Pi_i / \partial p_j$ with respect to p_l ($l \neq j$):

$$
\begin{aligned}
\frac{\partial^2 \Pi_i}{\partial p_j \partial p_l} &= \frac{\partial \pi_{ij}}{\partial p_l} \cdot \frac{\partial \Pi_i}{\partial p_j} \cdot \frac{1}{\pi_{ij}} + \pi_{ij} \alpha_i \cdot \frac{\Psi_{ij}}{\varsigma_{ij}} \cdot \frac{\partial \Pi_i}{\partial p_l} \\
&= \alpha_i \cdot \left(\pi_{il} \frac{\Psi_{il}}{\varsigma_{il}} \cdot \frac{\partial \Pi_i}{\partial p_j} + \pi_{ij} \frac{\Psi_{ij}}{\varsigma_{ij}} \cdot \frac{\partial \Pi_i}{\partial p_l} \right) \quad ,
\end{aligned}
\tag{3.29}
$$

and the Hessian of $\Pi(\mathbf{A}, \mathbf{p}, \mathbf{y}, \alpha)$ is symmetric. Proceeding similarly, the second partial of $\partial \Pi_i / \partial p_j$ with respect to p_j is:

$$
\begin{aligned}
\frac{\partial^2 \Pi_i}{\partial p_j^2} &= \alpha_i (2\pi_{ij} - 1) \frac{\Psi_{ij}}{\varsigma_{ij}} \cdot \frac{\partial \Pi_i}{\partial p_j} + \alpha_i \pi_{ij} \left(\frac{\Psi_{ij}^2}{\varsigma_{ij}^2} - \frac{\psi_{ij}}{\varsigma_{ij}} \right) (\Pi_i - (p_j - c_{ij}) \Psi_{ij}) \\
&+ \alpha_i \pi_{ij} \frac{\Psi_{ij}}{\varsigma_{ij}} ((p_j - c_{ij}) \psi_{ij} - \Psi_{ij}) - \pi_{ij} \left(2\psi_{ij} - (p_j - c_{ij}) \frac{\partial \psi_{ij}}{\partial p_j} \right) \quad , (3.30)
\end{aligned}
$$

and the coefficients of the Hessian matrix of the profit function Π are:

$$\frac{\partial^2 \Pi(\mathbf{A}, \mathbf{p}, \mathbf{y}, \alpha)}{\partial p_j \partial p_l} = \sum_{i=1}^{n} N_i \cdot \frac{\partial^2 \Pi_i(\mathbf{A}, \mathbf{p}, \mathbf{y}, \alpha_i)}{\partial p_j \partial p_l} \quad , \tag{3.31}$$

$$\frac{\partial^2 \Pi(\mathbf{A}, \mathbf{p}, \mathbf{y}, \alpha)}{\partial p_j^2} = \sum_{i=1}^{n} N_i \cdot \frac{\partial^2 \Pi_i(\mathbf{A}, \mathbf{p}, \mathbf{y}, \alpha_i)}{\partial p_j^2} \quad . \tag{3.32}$$

If the α_i's tends to zero, all non-diagonal elements of the Hessian of $\Pi_i(\mathbf{A}, \mathbf{p}, \mathbf{y}, \alpha_i)$ are close to zero. For the diagonal elements we find:

$$\lim_{\alpha_i \to 0} \frac{\partial^2 \Pi_i(\mathbf{A}, \mathbf{p}, \mathbf{y}, \alpha_i)}{\partial p_j^2} = -\pi_{ij} \left(2\psi_{ij} - (p_j - c_{ij}) \frac{\partial \psi_{ij}}{\partial p_j} \right) \quad . \tag{3.33}$$

Hence, in general we can not assume that our problem is concave, not even, if the behavior shows a high degree of randomness (α small). However, if we assume that the reservation price of segment i and bundle j is normally distributed with mean μ_{ij} and standard deviation σ_{ij}, (3.33) modifies to

$$\lim_{\alpha_i \to 0} \frac{\partial^2 \Pi_i(\mathbf{A}, \mathbf{p}, \mathbf{y}, \alpha_i)}{\partial p_j^2} = -\pi_{ij} \psi_{ij} \left(2 - (p_j - c_{ij}) \cdot \frac{p_j - \mu_{ij}}{\sigma_{ij}} \right) \quad . \tag{3.34}$$

A necessary and sufficient concavity condition for a diagonal matrix is that all diagonal elements are negative. With respect to segment i, the diagonal element j of the Hessian of Π_i is negative, iff

$$p_j < \frac{\mu_{ij} + c_{ij}}{2} + \sqrt{\frac{(\mu_{ij} - c_{ij})^2}{4} + 2\sigma_{ij}} \quad , \tag{3.35}$$

or less restrictive $p_j \leq \mu_{ij}$. Hence, with respect to (3.32), for normally distributed reservation prices and sufficiently small values of α_i our problem will be concave, if the bundle prices are low enough to achieve a high penetration among the large customer segments. Since we can not a priori ensure the above condition, any potential solution method must be able to handle non-concave functions. In the following section, we present a strategy which is superior to any standard non-linear programming technique in finding the global optimum of a non-concave objective.

3.4.3 Homotopy and Bifurcation Theory Results

In this section we will define the homotopy terminology for continuous functions. A homotopy of two "smooth" functions can be viewed as a continuous transformation of their images using a family of functions with the cardinality of the continuum. For all considerations, we will exclusively use the Euclidean topology $\mathcal{E}$ which is induced by the Euclidean distance metric. Let f and g be two continuous functions from $\mathcal{R}^n$ to $\mathcal{R}$. A continuous mapping $H : (0; 1) \times \mathcal{R}^n \longrightarrow \mathcal{R}$ is called a *homotopy* between f and g, if $H(0, x) = f(x)$ and $H(1, x) = g(x)$ for all $x \in \mathcal{R}^n$. f and g are the called *homotope*. It is easy to see that the relation "homotope" is an equivalence relation for a set of continuous functions from $\mathcal{R}^n$ to $\mathcal{R}$. The elements of the corresponding quotient set are called *homotopy classes*. Homotopy theory is an advanced discipline of topological algebra. For a thorough and detailed analysis refer to Schubert (1969), Fréchet and Fan (1967), Aleksandrov (1965) or Hu (1959), among many others.

Using a homotopy H in terms of a parameter $\lambda \in (0, 1)$, we want to define a homotopy class, such that $H(1, \mathbf{p})$ gives us our original problem. We want $H(0, \mathbf{p})$ to be a "friendly" function, e.g. concave with a well-known maximum price vector. This price vector can be used as an initial vector to estimate the optimal price vector of $H(\varepsilon, \mathbf{p})$. For a sufficiently small step size $\varepsilon > 0$, we intend to drag along our path from maximum to maximum. Similar to the idea of Hanson and Martin (1994), we want to find a good-natured approximation of the alpha choice function $\pi_{ij}(\mathbf{A}, \mathbf{p}, \mathbf{y}, \alpha_i)$. Braibant and Fleury (1985) suggest a convex linearization which can easily be reversed to a concave linearization method. For an objective function f, the concave approximation f_C at a point $\mathbf{x}_0$ is defined by

$$f_C(\mathbf{x}) = f(\mathbf{x}_0) + \sum_{i=1}^{n} \delta_i (x_i - x_{0i}) \cdot \frac{\partial f(\mathbf{x}_0)}{\partial \mathbf{x}} \quad , \tag{3.36}$$

where

$$\delta_i = \begin{cases} 1 & \text{if } x_{0i}(\partial f/\partial x_i) \leq 0, \\ x_{0i}/x_i & \text{otherwise .} \end{cases} \tag{3.37}$$

However, to limit the number of function calls in view of computational effort we will not follow this approach. Instead we will choose a rational polynomial of low degree as an approximation of the choice rule. In the modified choice function demand for bundle j is decoupled from the demand for other bundles. To maintain a similar scaling, the modified demand function and the alpha rule function coincide at the upper price bound $\mathbf{u}$. For a fixed reference price vector $\mathbf{r} = (r_1, \ldots, r_m)$, we define

$$\tilde{\pi}_{ij}(\mathbf{p}) = \frac{1}{\Psi_{ij}(p_j)(p_j - c_{ij})} \cdot \left(a_2 p_j^2 + a_1 p_j + a_0 \right) \quad , \tag{3.38}$$

where

$$a_2 \;<\; 0$$

$$a_1 = -2a_2 r_j$$

$$a_0 = (u_j - c_{ij})\pi_{ij}(u_j) - a_2 u_j^2 - a_1 u_j \quad . \tag{3.39}$$

The magnitude of a_2 is not yet determined and can be used to scale the approximation appropriately. The fixed parameters $\mathbf{A}, \mathbf{y}$, and α are here omitted for ease of notation. We will now define our homotopy as a combination of the original profit function and the profit function with modified choice behavior:

$$H_i(\lambda, \mathbf{p}) = \sum_{j=1}^m (p_j - c_{ij})\left(\lambda \pi_{ij} + (1 - \lambda)\tilde{\pi}_{ij}\right)\Psi_{ij}(p_j) \quad , \tag{3.40}$$

and

$$H(\lambda, \mathbf{p}) = \sum_{i=1}^n N_i H_i(\lambda) \quad . \tag{3.41}$$

For each λ we have

$$H(\lambda, \mathbf{p}) = \lambda H(1, \mathbf{p}) + (1 - \lambda) H(0, \mathbf{p}) \quad , \tag{3.42}$$

$$\lim_{\delta \to 0} H(\lambda + \delta, \mathbf{p}) = H(\lambda, \mathbf{p}) \quad , \tag{3.43}$$

for all $\mathbf{p}$, hence H is continuous on $(0;1)$. H is a homotopy between our original, in general non-concave profit function $\Pi(\mathbf{A}, \mathbf{p}, \mathbf{y}, \alpha) = H(1, \mathbf{p})$ and

$$H(0, \mathbf{p}) = \sum_{i=1}^n \sum_{j=1}^m N_i \, (p_j - c_{ij}) \, \tilde{\pi}_{ij} \Psi_{ij}(p_j) \quad . \tag{3.44}$$

It is easy to see that $H(0, \mathbf{u}) = H(1, \mathbf{u})$, and $H(0, \mathbf{p})$ is a strictly concave function which attains its global maximum at $\mathbf{p} = \mathbf{r}$:

$$\frac{\partial H_i(0, \mathbf{p})}{\partial p_j} = 2a_2 \cdot (p_j - r_j) \quad (j = 1, \ldots, m)$$

$$\frac{\partial^2 H_i(0, \mathbf{p})}{\partial p_j \partial p_l} = 0 \quad (l \neq j)$$

$$\frac{\partial^2 H_i(0, \mathbf{p})}{\partial p_j^2} = 2a_2 < 0 \quad . \tag{3.45}$$

Our next goal is to show that information on extremal behavior of any member $H(\lambda, \mathbf{p})$ of the homotopy class can be "transported" to $H(\lambda + \varepsilon, \mathbf{p})$ if $\varepsilon > 0$ is small enough. A necessary condition for the existence of an extreme point is that all partial derivatives with respect to price are zero. Our goal is to locally characterize the behavior of extremal points as functions of λ, such that extreme points can only change within a predictable range as we increase λ to $\lambda + \varepsilon$ for all $\lambda \in [0; 1)$. Unfortunately, the system

$$\nabla_p h(\lambda, \mathbf{p}) = 0 \quad , \tag{3.46}$$

is non-linear for all $\lambda \in (0; 1]$ due to the non-linear alpha choice rule. Thus, it is not possible to solve the system directly. However, we can describe the local behavior of (3.46) near any regular point (Figure 3.10).

Figure 3.10: Local Resolution of $F(x) = 0$

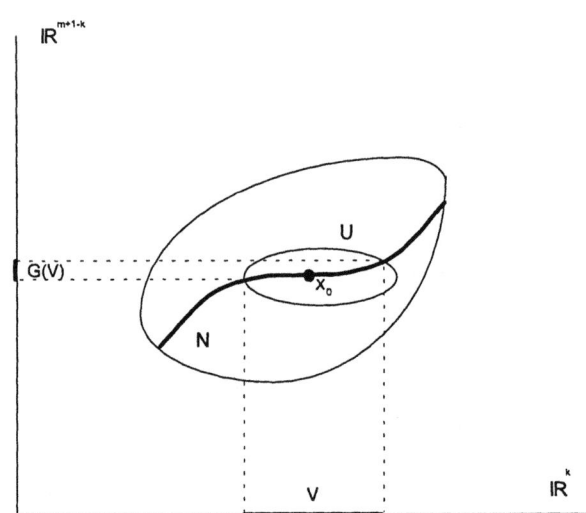

Formally, we will use the classic implicit function theorem (see Dieudonné, 1969):

Implicit Function Theorem 5: Let $k < m + 1$, $M \subseteq \mathcal{R}^{m+1}$ open, $F \in \mathcal{C}^p(M, \mathcal{R}^k)$ for some $p \geq 1$ and define $N = \{\mathbf{x} \in \mathcal{R}^{m+1} \,|\, F(\mathbf{x}) = 0\}$. Let $\mathbf{x}_0 \in N$ and the Jacobian matrix

$$DF(\mathbf{x}_0) = \begin{pmatrix} \partial F_1(\mathbf{x}_0)/\partial x_1 & \cdots & \partial F_1(\mathbf{x}_0)/\partial x_k \\ \cdots & \ddots & \cdots \\ \partial F_m(\mathbf{x}_0)/\partial x_1 & \cdots & \partial F_m(\mathbf{x}_0)/\partial x_k \end{pmatrix} \tag{3.47}$$

be of full rank. Then, there exists an open neighborhood U of $\mathbf{x}_0$ in M, an open set $V \subseteq \mathcal{R}^{m+1-k}$ and a function $G \in \mathcal{C}^p(V, \mathcal{R}^k)$ with $N \cap U = \{(v, G(v)) \mid \forall v \in V\}$.

The following proposition is an immediate conclusion of the implicit function theorem:

Proposition 6: Let $\lambda_0 \in I = (0,1)$, $\mathbf{p}^0 = (p_1^0, \ldots, p_m^0)$ a price vector, such that $\nabla_p H(\lambda_0, \mathbf{p}^0) = 0$. Furthermore, let $Hess(H(\lambda, \mathbf{p}))$ be regular at $(\lambda_0, \mathbf{p}^0)$. Then there is a $\varepsilon > 0$, continuously differentiable functions h_j on $(\lambda_0 - \varepsilon, \lambda_0 + \varepsilon) \cap I$, such that $p_j^0 = h_j(\lambda_0)$ and $\nabla_p H(\lambda, h_1(\lambda), \ldots, h_m(\lambda)) = 0$ for all $\lambda \in (\lambda_0 - \varepsilon, \lambda_0 + \varepsilon) \cap I$.

The proposition is not constructive in the sense, that it doesn't tell us how the local resolutions h_j look alike and whether we can choose a ε independent of λ as a global stepsize. However, the following Lemma tells that as long as we avoid singular points, there will always be a constant stepsize $\bar{\varepsilon} > 0$, such that our algorithm terminates after $\lceil \frac{1}{\bar{\varepsilon}} \rceil + 1$ steps.

Lemma 7: Let $(\lambda_k, \mathbf{p}^k)$ a sequence of extreme points of H with $\lambda_k < \lambda_{k+1}$ for all k. Then there exists $\lambda_0 < 1$ with $\lambda_k \to \lambda_0$, $p_j^0 = \lim_{k \to \infty} p_j^k$ exists for all $j \leq m$ and $Hess(H(\lambda, \mathbf{p}))$ at $(\lambda_0, \mathbf{p}^0)$ is singular for $\mathbf{p}^0 = (p_1^0, \ldots, p_m^0)$.

Proof: Since (λ_k) is a monotone and bounded sequence of real numbers, there is a $\lambda_0 < 1$ with $\lim_{k \to \infty} \lambda_k = \lambda_0$. From the proposition above we know, that all local resolutions $p_j^k = h_j(\lambda_k)$ are continuous and hence $\lim_{k \to \infty} p_j^k$ exists for all $j \leq m$. If $\mathbf{p}^0$ were a regular point of $H(\lambda_0)$, another application of the implicit function theorem would yield a new neighborhood $[\lambda_0, \lambda_0 + \varepsilon_{k+1})$ to proceed.$\square$

Another pitfall which could cause our path search to be misdirected to a poor local optimum of $H(1)$ are so-called bifurcation points (see Figure 3.11). Let $S = \{(\mathbf{p}, \lambda) \mid \nabla_p H(\lambda, \mathbf{p}) = 0\}$. $(\lambda_0, \mathbf{p}^0)$ is called a *bifurcation point of the equation* $\nabla_p H(\lambda, \mathbf{p}) = 0$, if (1) $(\lambda_0, \mathbf{p}^0) \in S$ and (2) for all neighborhoods U of $\mathbf{p}^0$, Λ of λ_0 and $\mathbf{p}^1, \mathbf{p}^2 \in U$, we have $\mathbf{p}^1 \neq \mathbf{p}^2$ and $(\lambda_0, \mathbf{p}^1), (\lambda_0, \mathbf{p}^2) \in S$. If we run into a bifurcation point during a search step, there is no way to decide which path leads to the optimal answer. The following bifurcation theorem tells us that again bifurcation

Figure 3.11: Bifurcation Point of $H(\lambda, x)$

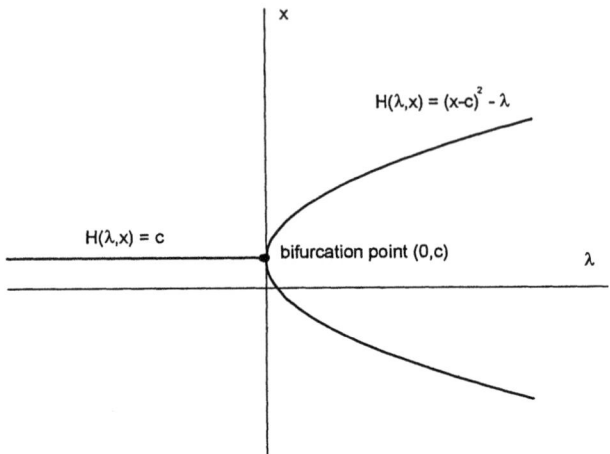

points can only be singular points of $H(\lambda)$.

Bifurcation Theorem 8: Let $\Lambda = (\lambda_k - \varepsilon, \lambda_k + \varepsilon) \cap (0,1)$ for a $\lambda_k \in (0,1)$ and $\varepsilon > 0$. Let U be a neighborhood of $\mathbf{p}^k$ and $\nabla_p H(\lambda_k, \mathbf{p}^k) = 0$. Let the Hessian of $H(\lambda_k, \mathbf{p}^k)$ be continuous at $(\lambda_0, \mathbf{p}^0) \in \Lambda \times U$ and $\mathbf{p}^0$ is a regular point of H. Then, $(\lambda_0, \mathbf{p}^0)$ is no bifurcation point.

Proof: If the inverse of the Hessian of $H(\lambda_k, \mathbf{p}^k)$ is a bijection at $(\lambda_0, \mathbf{p}^0)$, Banach's Open Mapping Theorem (see Yosida, 1965) tells that the Hessian of $H(\lambda_k, \mathbf{p}^k)$ is a topological isomorphism. Applying the implicit function theorem again, there exists a neighborhood $\Lambda_0 \times U_0 \subset \Lambda \times U$ of $(\lambda_0, \mathbf{p}^0)$ such that the equation $\nabla_p H(\lambda, \mathbf{p}) = 0$ for each $\lambda \in \Lambda_0$ has a unique solution in U_0. Hence, $(\lambda_0, \mathbf{p}^0)$ can not be a bifurcation point.$\Box$

Thus, any point $(\lambda_0, \mathbf{p}^0)$ can only be a bifurcation point of $\nabla_p H(\lambda, \mathbf{p}) = 0$, if 0 is an eigenvalue of $Hess(H(\lambda, \mathbf{p}))$ at $(\lambda_0, \mathbf{p}_0)$.

We know now that once we have found a maximum of one of our profit functions $H(\lambda)$, the corresponding maximum price vector in most cases provides a good starting point for the optimization of a subsequent profit function $H(\lambda + \varepsilon)$. We emphasize that there is no guarantee that our optimization approach will find the global maximum of our initial profit function because we are not protected against encountering singular points. A way to build confidence in the presented method is to vary the stepsize and the still not specified reference price vector $\mathbf{r}$. If several choices of $(\varepsilon, \mathbf{r})$ give us the same resulting optimal price vector for our bundle profit function, we can be rather sure that we are truly optimal.

3.4.4 Collecting Data

This section deals with the question how to find the utility, i.e., reservation price distributions for the considered bundles across all customer segments, and how to determine the degree of randomness α in customers choice behavior. Although Gabor and Granger (1966) suggest a lognormal distribution of maximum prices for homogeneous customer groups, we will assume that the reservation price for each bundle and customer segment follows a normal distribution for two main reasons (following Kohli and Mahajan, 1991):

- A consumer's reservation price reflects the marginal value of a bundle in relation to the value of all other offers. Thus, we need to be able to take into account both positive and negative reservation prices. The phenomenon of strong dislike of certain options is well-known in the automobile industry. Some customers, for instance, are strictly averse to air-conditioning which would correspond to a negative reservation price. A normal distribution retains this advantage over many other models (e.g. lognormal or exponential distributions) that are restricted to positive reservation prices.

- A normal distribution provides a flexible mean to approximate skewed reservation price distributions. If an empirical distribution is, for instance, skewed to the right, it can't be approximated by a lognormal distribution.

Hence, for each segment i and bundle j we let

$$\psi_{ij}(p_j) = \frac{1}{\sqrt{2\pi}\sigma_{ij}} \cdot \exp\left(-\frac{(p_j - \mu_{ij})^2}{2\sigma_{ij}^2}\right) \quad . \tag{3.48}$$

From our sales data, we can extract "truncated" information on the reservation price distribution for each segment and bundle. At the particular price, a combination of options was offered, we know the penetration, i.e., for one year the V6 engine and automatic drive were offered at an aggregated price p, and 65% of the "luxury" segment purchased it. The pair $(p, .65)$ gives us a "point" on the trace of the reservation price distribution for the particular segment and bundle. If we discount prices of different ages for each bundle/segment combination, we can obtain several points. In addition, we will assume a 1% and a 99% price threshold to provide a lower (which may be negative) and upper truncation of the reservation price distribution.

Figure 3.12: Error Distribution for (μ, σ) sweep for three pairs

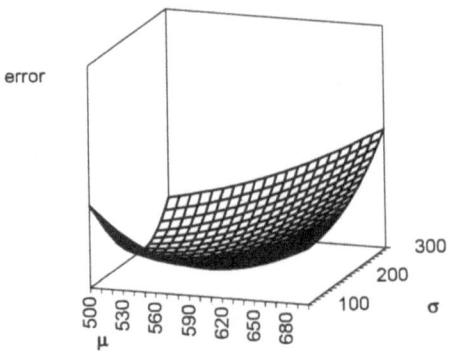

For a pair (i,j) and K_{ij} corresponding price/penetration combinations (p_{jk}, ρ_{ijk}) $(k = 1, \ldots, K_{ij})$, we minimize the least squares

$$\sum_{k=1}^{K_{ij}} \left(\frac{1}{\sqrt{2\pi}\sigma_{ij}} \cdot \exp\left(-\frac{(p_{jk} - \mu_{ij})^2}{2\sigma_{ij}^2}\right) - \rho_{ijk} \right)^2 \tag{3.49}$$

with respect to σ_{ij} and μ_{ij}. Simulation shows that usually four pairs (p, ρ) are sufficient to find a "sharp" minimum, if prices p_{jk} are not "too" close. Three pairs are usually not sufficient (see Figures 3.12, 3.13). Price changes for options and option combinations thus can be used to add new price/penetration pairs and obtain better fits for (μ_{ij}, σ_{ij}).

Figure 3.13: Error Distribution for (μ, σ) sweep for four pairs

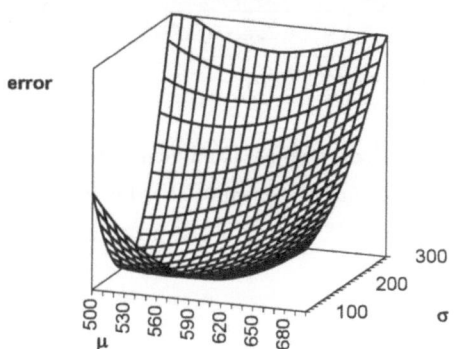

To estimate the choice variable α_i for each customer segment i, we proceed in a similar way. Using the above reservation price distributions, we can compute the corresponding surpluses ς_{ij} by (3.3). For each segment i, we normalize the according penetrations, such that for all $k = 1, \ldots, K_{ij}$

$$\sum_{j=1}^{m+m^*} \rho_{ijk} = 1 \quad . \tag{3.50}$$

Figure 3.14: Error Distribution for an α sweep

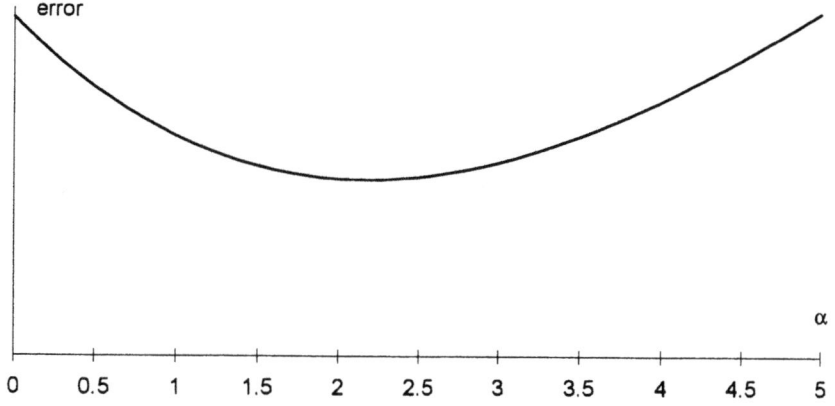

For each triple $(p_{jk}, \rho_{ijk}; \varsigma_{ij}(p_k))$, we minimize

$$\sum_{j=1}^{m+m^*} \sum_{k=1}^{K_{ij}} \left(\frac{\varsigma_{ij}^{\alpha_i}(p_{jk})}{\bar{\varsigma}_i^{\alpha_i} + \sum_{j=1}^{m} \varsigma_{ij}^{\alpha_i}(p_{jk})} \cdot \Psi_{ij}(p_{jk}) - \rho_{ijk} \right)^2 \tag{3.51}$$

for each segment i with respect to α_i.

For a fixed scenario of prices, surpluses and penetrations, Figure 3.14 shows the error term of the above least square procedure as a function of α_i. For each segment i, we will use now the estimations of α_i as last missing parameter for the alpha choice rule.

3.5   A Heuristic Decomposition Algorithm for the SBP

In this section we will present a heuristic algorithm which is based on decomposing the SBP problem in a mixed-linear integer program and a non-linear program. The first problem will be solved using a greedy closed method, similar to the one presented in chapter one. The non-linear non-concave problem is solved using the presented homotopy approach, where at each step we use the gradient projection method of Rosen (1960) to solve the non-linear program with linear constraints.

We assume that we already have a pool of candidate bundles by solving the buyer's problem (3.10). Then, we decompose the original SBP problem (3.15) in a mixed linear integer

Master Problem (M):

Objective

$$\max \quad -\sum_{j=1}^{m} f_j y_j + \theta \quad , \tag{3.52}$$

subject to

$$\sum_{j=1}^{m} y_j = m_0 \quad , \tag{3.53}$$

$$y_j \in \{0,1\} \quad j = 1,\ldots,m \quad , \tag{3.54}$$

and either

$$a_{kj} \cdot (y_k + y_j) \leq 1 \quad k = 1,\ldots,r, \; j = r+1,\ldots,m \quad , \tag{3.55}$$

$$\sum_{j=1}^{m} x_{kj} y_j \geq 1 \quad k = 1,\ldots,r \quad , \tag{3.56}$$

or

$$y_j = 1 \quad \forall \, j = 1,\ldots,r \quad , \tag{3.57}$$

and a non-linear

Subproblem (S):

$$\theta = \max \sum_{i=1}^{n} N_i \Pi_i(\mathbf{A}, \mathbf{p}, \mathbf{y}, \alpha_i) \quad , \tag{3.58}$$

subject to

$$0 \leq p_j \leq u_j \quad j = 1,\ldots,m \quad . \tag{3.59}$$

To solve the two-level problem, we start with the vector $\mathbf{y} = (1, 1, \ldots, 1)$ and produce each bundle. In the subproblem, we solve the non-linear pricing problem using the homotopy approach (HA) together with Rosen's gradient projection method (GPR) at each search step. In the next stage, we will increase the number of offered bundles by the one which produces the highest profit contribution by solving the non-linear subproblem. We will proceed until the number of produced bundles reaches m_0.

<u>SBP Algorithm:</u>

Step 1 (Initialize):
Stepsize for homotopy method ε and linearization vector $\mathbf{r}$. Product line (all single options produced) $(y_1, \ldots, y_r, y_{r+1}, \ldots, y_m) = (1, \ldots, 1, 0, \ldots, 0)$.
Start price vector $\mathbf{p}^0 = (p_1^0, \ldots, p_m^0)$, $z^* = -\infty$.

Step 2 (Loop):
For $k = 1, \ldots, m_0$
For $j = 1, \ldots, k$

Step 3 (Optimization):

If $y_j = 0$ then let $\hat{\mathbf{y}} = (y_1, \ldots, y_{j-1}, 1, y_{j+1}, \ldots, y_m)$.

$z = max\ \Pi(\mathbf{A}, \mathbf{p}, \hat{\mathbf{y}}, \alpha)$. Else, goto step 5.

Step 4 (Optimality Check):

If $z > z^*$ and $\hat{\mathbf{y}}$ is feasible then let $\mathbf{y} = \hat{\mathbf{y}}$ and $z^* = z$.

Step 5 (Loop):

Next j

Next k

The subproblem (S) is solved $(m - \frac{m_0}{2})(m_0 + 1)$ times. Each subproblem call implies $\lceil \frac{1}{\varepsilon} \rceil + 1$ calls of the non-linear search method. Although we expect the GPR to find the optimum of the current function $H(\lambda)$ within one or two steps due to a good starting vector, a robust and reliable univariate line-search method for the Gradient Projection method is crucial. A second factor which mainly determines the runtime effort of the algorithm, is the numerical integration method we use to compute surplus and density. In the next section we will analyze the performance of the presented algorithm for an example using current data of a German automobile producer.

3.6   Computational Results

The data to test our optimization procedure is taken from the Opel ASTRA GL which is the base model of the European successor of the Pontiac LeMans, and is available as 3-door limousine, 4-door sedan/5-door limousine, and wagon. In 1993, the Adam Opel AG sold 307,291 units on the European market with shares of 25%, 45% and 30% for the different body styles, which were regarded as customer segments during the optimization.

All presented methods were implemented in FORTRAN77 and have been run on a Siemens/Nixdorf 486 PC with a math co-processor. The respective steps and the result of the optimization can easily be tracked and processed by a spreadsheet as Microsoft EXCEL, for instance.

At first, we applied the forecast disaggregation method to generate a car pool with forecast character which is the base data for our subsequent analyses. The corresponding linear program was solved with the Simplex method. The forecast disaggregation method proved to be very reliable in terms of ex-ante-fit: at the option level, the resulting forecast car pool shows a mean relative error of 0.35% with a maximum relative error of 1.19%. Figure 3.15 shows the essential problem parameters and computation effort.

Figure 3.15: Problem Parameters for Forecast Disaggregation

Number of Car Types	Number of Forecasts	Objective Value	CPU time (secs.)
6,024	44	15.42	62.45

We have now selected ten comfort/safety options and estimated their part-worths running a conjoint analysis of the disaggregated forecast car pool. These part-worths vary between +0.47 (heat absorbing glass) and -0.41 (check control). We chose all bundles with aggregated part worths ≥ 0.2 which happened to be twelve. Figure 3.16 shows a list of the problem parameters and computation time.

Figure 3.16: Problem Parameters for Buyer's Problem

Number of Bundles	Number of Segments	Number of Options	Number of LAR constraints	CPU time (secs.)
1,024	3	10	62	2.31

The next step was to determine the option demand structure for each of the three segments in terms of reservation price distribution and randomness of choice α by least square methods. The choice parameters we found for the three segments were 0.686, 0.689 and 0.832, respectively, which means a relatively high degree of randomness in option choice behavior. With these values for α, the choice model is able to approximate the option market conditions of the 1993 Opel ASTRA sales with a mean relative error of 5.4%. From this example and others, choice behavior turned out to be more random for low-price segments than for higher priced trim levels.

Finally, we determined the variable cost of each option/segment and bundle/segment combination, as well as the single option fix cost. To estimate the fix cost associated with a bundle, we need to distinguish between a mixed and a pure bundling strategy. For mixed bundling, there is no savings due to safety stock reduction or deprolife-ration, since each option can still be ordered individually. Thus, the fix costs for a bundle were estimated as the sum of fix costs of the included single options. For pure bundling, we expressed the pooling and process deproliferation effect in terms of bundle j fix costs f_j by

$$f_j = \left(\sum_{t=1}^{r} x_{tj} f_t^2 \right)^{1/2} .$$

(3.60)

The optimization procedure was now run for a mixed and a pure bundling strategy, considering up to five ($=m_0$) common optimal bundles for all segments. To evaluate the quality of the results, we used total enumeration instead of the greedy heuristic and repeated the computations on a CRAY YMP 2-32. Figure 3.17 shows all relevant problem parameters and effort/accuracy measures. For this example, we chose a stepsize of 0.2 for the homotopy method. However, the quality of the results did not change as we increased the stepsize up to one. Thus, for small α values, the problem shows a high degree of concavity. Furthermore, it is interesting that in the pure bundling case the quality of the optimum for five bundles allowed (94.2%) is superior to the quality of the optimum in the case of four bundles allowed (92.1%). Apparently, the greedy heuristic got stuck in a local optimum in the case of four pure bundles allowed. In general, however, there seems to be no significant difference in terms of quality of optimum between a pure and a mixed bundling strategy which decreases, if the number of bundles allowed is increased. In Figure 3.18, we show the maximum profit obtained by each bundling strategy as a function of the number of bundles.

At first, it should be remarked that mixed bundling is the most profitable bundling strategy, although it does not support deproliferation at all. The profit obtained

Figure 3.17: Problem Parameters for the Stochastic Bundle Optimization

Number of Pure Bundles	CPU time (secs.)	Quality of Optimum in %
1	4.1	100.0
2	16.8	100.0
3	64.5	99.1
4	169.4	92.1
5	298.7	94.2

Number of Mixed Bundles	CPU time (secs.)	Quality of Optimum in %
1	8.8	100.0
2	38.8	100.0
3	101.9	100.0
4	222.1	98.0
5	386.2	94.3

by two optimal bundles is approximately 34% higher than for unbundled sales. In general, profit for mixed bundling does not change a lot with the number of bundles. In the pure bundling case, profit decreases with growing number of bundles. The reason is that all candidate bundles contain hot seller options which yielded high single option profit before. Penetrations for the pure bundles however are lower, such that the lost single option profit can not be outweighed by higher demand for low runner options within a bundle. Nevertheless, one optimal pure bundle is still 5% more profitable than unbundled sales in this case.

Both bundling strategies show a certain trend for hierarchy with regard to the bundles which are optimal with respect to a fixed number of bundles to be chosen (m_0). An optimal bundle for a small m_0 is frequently also optimal for a strategy with larger m_0. This property is more pronounced for pure bundling than for mixed bundling, since in a mixed bundling strategy, each bundle not only competes with other bundles but also with all single options which are part of the bundle. This

Figure 3.18: Maximum Profit for Different Numbers of Bundles

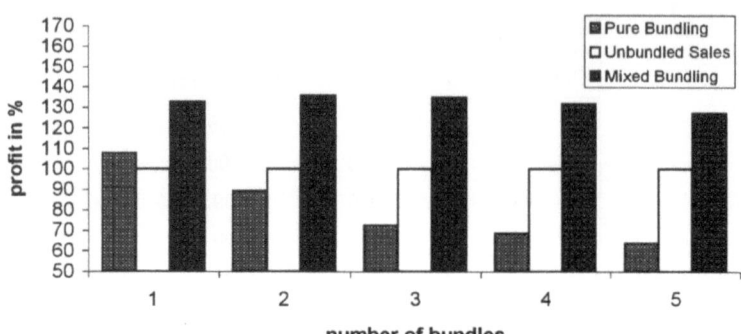

hierarchy property supports the utilized greedy heuristic which tends to preserve each bundle which was part of the optimal solution at some iteration step.

For both strategies, the resulting optimal prices are usually decreasing with increasing number of optimal bundles. The proposed discounts for the bundles vary between 15 and 35% of the single option prices. Although optimal prices for comparable bundles are slightly higher in a pure bundling strategy, penetrations of bundles are higher as well due to the missing competition with free-flow options. Furthermore, we have performed a Monte Carlo simulation with the cost and demand data of the above example to assess the dependency of the potential profit from each bundling strategy on the randomness of choice. For this purpose, we randomly generated 500 α values for each of the three segments, which were equally distributed in the interval $[0.5; 1.5]$. Demand structures of various car segments that we have analyzed could be described by α values which fall in the mentioned range. For each of the 500 combinations we ran the simulation to determine the optimal profit for mixed and pure bundling. As an aggregated measure for the choice randomness we took the Euclidean norm of the three α's:

$$\bar{\alpha} = \sqrt{\alpha_1^2 + \alpha_2^2 + \alpha_3^2} \quad . \tag{3.61}$$

It is remarkable that maximum profit for mixed bundling is increasing as choice behavior gets less random, while maximum profit for pure bundling is decreasing, as to be seen in Figure 3.19. In general, the resulting changes are small and almost linear, while the optimal number of bundles for each strategy is not affected at all.

In addition to the conventional wisdom about bundling, the simulations with real data disclosed a couple of new opportunities and caveats. Some of the presented insights are problem specific, others could be generalized by numerous computational examples. Although an analytical optimization is inevitable to fully exploit an option bundling strategy, we finally try to "translate" the most important numerical results into guidelines which may serve management as conceptual rules-of-thumb.

Figure 3.19: Sensitivity of Profit With Respect to Choice Randomness

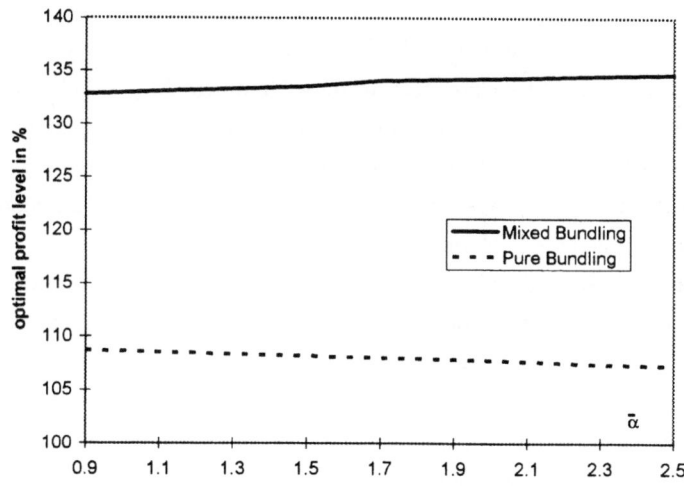

Composition of the Bundle:

A bundle should contain one or two high runner options which provide a certain share level. In turn, more than four options in a bundle may be too difficult to survey or too specific for the customer and thus are share reducing. Frequently, a profitable bundle can be designed by adding on new options to an already existing and successful bundle. Cost synergies among options are almost always worth to be considered.

Bundle Price:

The bundle price should express the price level of the segment that it is targeted for. Low price segments are rather assigned inexpensive, thus not too comprehensive bundles. Bundle discounts are frequently "reasonable" between 15 and 30%. However, since profit has been proved to be sensitive to product price changes, the bundle price should always be the result of an analytical optimization. Finally it is very important that the customer actually realizes the granted discount on each bundle.

Form of Bundling:

If option postponement is not part of the manufacturers business policy, mixed bundling is generally to be preferred to pure bundling. In particular, if the cost structure is not appropriate to account for cost savings due to deproliferation, pure bundling will hardly prove to be more profitable than mixed bundling. In addition, mixed bundling is always demand enhancing, whereas pure bundling may limit supply for the customer. Moreover, it is very likely for a car producer that pure bundling is no feasible global strategy and unbundling is enforced by local markets. Hence, no synergy cost advantages can be exploited, if the concerning car model is manufactured in one "home" plant.

In pure bundling, one common bundle for all segments is frequently desirable. Under a mixed bundling strategy, profit does not show to be very sensitive to the number of bundles; however, most examples we have analyzed revealed an optimal number of one bundle per segment.

In General:

Bundling has shown to be always more profitable than unbundled sales. Option profit increases of more than 30% are common. Furthermore, the option choice behavior of almost all considered customer segments shows a rather high degree of randomness. Thus, choice behavior is not very much affected by conceptual changes: a customer is not likely to switch from Chrysler to Ford, because he can not buy his car in "lifestyle blue" or because dual airbags are made standard even for the low trim levels. However, whether a customer is inclined to trade up or to trade down his option equipment can only be found out by a simulation.

3.7 Summary

In the third chapter, we have motivated and surveyed various bundling strategies with a focus on the automobile industry and studied the essential bundling literature. For the first time, a model has been developed which allows to find profit maximizing pure bundling and mixed bundling policies under uncertainty. The model has been formulated as a non-linear mixed-integer program which also takes into account fix costs. We have presented a decomposition method to solve the stochastic bundling problem and applied a path-finding technique to tackle non-concave settings which may lead to poor local maxima if traditional non-linear methods are utilized. The algorithm has been implemented on a PC 486 with co-processor in FORTRAN77.

We have tested the methodology with topical and complex datasets from the automobile industry and assessed the optimization process for a particular problem. Furthermore, we have tried to convert some of the experience gained from its numerical context into management guidelines.

The practical implementation of many theoretical product line design methods fails, because necessary input data is not available or of poor quality. Furthermore, far-reaching changes of the business process may deter management, in particular if presented in an intransparent and inflexible way. The presented methodology will be made available as a tool for the car platform managers at Opel to yield a high acceptance level from the beginning on. Computation times hardly exceed five minutes which guarantees on-line processing. All necessary input data stems from standard sources. The analytical description of the demand structure in terms of mean reservation prices and standard deviations, or randomness of choice behavior is performed internally. Therefore, we have avoided a cumbersome and expensive data collection process by exploiting all internally available resources.

Although our considerations and findings mainly referred to an automotive background, there are no limitations of the presented methodology to a particular business branch. Bundling has become a widespread business policy and its benefits can be far-reaching. However, the potential profitability is too high to just view bundling as a commonsense marketing gimmick.

Chapter 4

Research Extensions

One focus of future work should be on improving the input car data which is an essential part of each optimization method presented. It is desirable to incorporate empirical data on lost sales due to a lack of customization into our disaggregated sales data which would approximate actual customer preferences more accurately.

In the field of complexity management, we want to expand our analytical methods to cross-car-line considerations, i.e., what is the potential of a high level of part convergence or even part commonality for a car producer? In terms of optimization methods, we do not know whether our heuristic approach is the best that exists. Consequently, more research in the field of method analysis and method evaluation needs to be done.

Future research in the field of option bundling should concentrate on the following aspects: how can mathematical techniques be employed to "dynamically" create bundles during the optimization procedure rather than to intelligently choose them from a given candidate pool? Is it possible to incorporate external competition and the downside risk associated with a bundling strategy into the model? What is the benefit of option bundling contrasted with other supply chain strategies, such as option postponement or maximum freedom of choice, in a global market environment?

Last not least, this mathematical method should also be experienced in the scope of combining product and services.

References

Adams, W.J. and Yellen, J.L., "Commodity Bundling and the Burden of Monopoly", *Quarterly Journal of Economics*, 90 (1976), 475-498.

Aleksandrov, P., *Combinatorial Topology*, Graylock Press, Baltimore (MD), 1965.

Allenby, G. and Rossi, P., "Quality Perceptions and Asymmetric Switching Between Brands", *Marketing Science*, 10 (1991), 185-204.

Anderson, P., "Wire Harness Testing", *Quality*, 21 (1982), 42-43.

Balas, E. and Ho, A., "Set Covering Algorithms Using Cutting Planes, Heuristics, and Subgradient Optimization: A Computational Study", *Mathematical Programming*, 12 (1980), 37-60.

Bauer, H., Herrmann, A. and Mengen, A., "Eine Methode zur gewinnmaximalen Produktgestaltung auf der Basis des Conjoint Measurement", *Zeitschrift für Betriebswirtschaft*, 64 (1994), 81-94.

Bazaraa, M.S., Sherali, H.D. and Shetty, C.M., *Nonlinear Programming*, Wiley Interscience Series in Discrete Mathematics and Optimization, New York, 1993.

Bechtold, S.E. and Jacobs, L.W., "Improvement of Labor Utilization in Shift Scheduling for Services with Implicit Optimal Modelling", *International Journal of Operations and Production Management*, 11 (1991), 54-69.

Beskow, W., Dichtl, E., Koeglmayr, H.G. and Raffée, H., "Faktisches Bestellverhalten als Grundlage einer optimalen Ausstattungspolitik bei Pkw-Modellen", *Zeitschrift für betriebswirtschaftliche Forschung*, 35 (1983), 173-196.

Blackstone, E.A., "Restrictive Practices in the Marketing of Electrofax Copying Machines and Supplies: The SCM Corporation Case", *Journal of Industrial Economics*, 23 (1975), 189-202.

Bozer, Y. and Srinivasan, M.M, "Tandem AGV Systems: A Partitioning Algorithm and Performance Comparison with Conventional AGV Systems", *European Journal of Operational Research*, 63 (1992), 173-191.

Bradley, S.P., Hax, A.C. and Magnanti, T.L., *Applied Mathematical Programming*, Addison–Wesley, Reading (MA), 1977.

Brown, G.G., Graves, G.W. and Ronen, D., "Scheduling Ocean Transportation of Crude Oil", *Management Science*, 33 (1987), 335-346.

Burstein, M.L., "The Economics of Tie–In Sales", *Review of Economics and Statistics*, 42 (1960), 68-73.

Burstein, M.L., "The Theory of Full–line Forcing", *Northwestern University Law Review*, 55 (1960), 62-95.

Cattin, P. and Wittink, D.R., "Commercial Use of Conjoint Analysis: An Update", *Journal of Marketing*, 53 (1989), 91-96.

Carbajo, J., De Meza, D. and Seidman, D.J., "A Strategic Motivation for Commodity Bundling", *Journal of Industrial Economics*, 38 (1990), 283-298.

Cattrysse, D., Salomon, M., Kuik, R. and Van Wassehove, L.N., "A dual ascent and column generation heuristic for the discrete lotsizing and scheduling problem with setup times", *Management Science*, 39 (1993), 477-486.

Coffman, E.G., Garey, M.R. and Johnson, D.S., "An Application of Bin-Packing to Multiprocessor Scheduling", *SIAM*, 7 (1978), 1-17.

Collins, N.E., Eglese, R.W. and Golden, B.L., "Simulated Annealing – and Annotated Bibliography", *American Journal of Mathematical Management Science*, 8 (1988), 209-308.

Connolly D., "General Purpose Simulated Annealing", *Journal of the Operational Research Society*, 43 (1992), 495-505.

Cornuejols, G., Fisher, M.L. and Nemhauser, G.L., "Location of Bank Accounts to Optimize Float: An Analytic Study of Exact and Approximate Algorithms", *Management Science*, 23 (1977), 789-810.

Cready, W.M., "Premium Bundling", *Economic Inquiry*, 29 (1991), 173-179.

Curry, D.J., *The New Marketing Research Systems: How to Use Strategic Database Information for Better Marketing Decisions*, John Wiley & Sons, New York, 1993.

Daganzo, C., *Multinomial Probit*, Academic Press, New York, 1979.

Dansby, R.E. and Conrad, C., "Commodity Bundling", *American Economic Review*, 74 (1984), 377-381.

Dantzig G.B., "Discrete Variable Extremum Problems", *Operations Research*, 5 (1957), 266-277.

Dantzig G.B. and Wolfe, P., "The Decomposition Algorithm for Linear Programming", *Operations Research*, 8 (1960), 101-111.

Dieudonné, J., *Foundations of Modern Analysis*, Academic Press, New York, 1969.

Dobson, G. and Kalish, S., "Positioning and Pricing a Product Line", *Marketing Science*, 7 (1988), 107-125.

Dobson, G. and Kalish, S., "Heuristics for Pricing and Positioning a Product–line Using Conjoint and Cost Data", *Management Science*, 39 (1993), 160-175.

Efroymson M. A. and Ray, T. L., "A Branch-Bound Algorithm for Plant Location", *Operations Research*, 14 (1966), 361-368.

El Darzi, E. and Mitra, G., "Solution of Set–Covering and Set–Partitioning Problems Using Assignment Relaxtions", *Journal of the Operational Research Society*, 43 (1992), 483-493.

Eppen, G.D., Hanson, W.A. and Martin, R.K., "Bundling – New Products, New Markets, Low Risk", *Sloan Management Review*, 32 (1991), 7-14.

Erlenkotter, D., "A Dual-Based Procedure for Uncapacitated Facility Location", *Operations Research*, 26 (1978), 992-1009.

Faaland, B. and Briggs, D., "Log Bucking and Lumber Manufacturing Using Dynamic Programming", *Management Science*, 30 (1984), 245-257.

Ferland, J.A. and Taillefer, S., "Vehicle Crew Scheduling to Complete Specific Tasks and Bulk–Tasks at Depots", *European Journal of Operational Research*, 57 (1992), 316-322.

Fisher, M.L., Kedia, P., "Optimal Solution of Set Covering/Partitioning Problems Using Dual Heuristics", *Management Science*, 36 (1990), 674-688.

Francis, R.L. and White, J.A., *Facility Layout and Location: An Analytical Approach*, Prentice–Hall, Englewood Cliffs (N.J.), 1974.

Francis, R.L., McGinnis, L.F. and White, J.A., "Locational Analysis", *European Journal of Operational Research*, 12 (1983), 220-252.

Frechet, M. and Fan, K., *Introduction to Combinatorial Topology*, Prindle, Weber & Smith, Boston (MA), 1967.

Fuerderer, R., *Invariante Zentrumsmannigfaltigkeiten*, Master Thesis, University of Freiburg, 1990.

Fuerderer, R., *Complexity Cost Control: Deproliferation of Wiring Harnesses at NUMMI*, GM Working Paper, 1993.

Gaeth, G.J., Levin, I.P., Chakraborty, G. and Levin, A.M., "Consumer Evaluation of Multi-Product Bundles: An Information Integration Analysis", *Marketing Letters*, 2 (1991), 47-57.

Garcia, C.B. and Zangwill, W.I., *Pathways to Solutions, Fixed Points and Equilibria*, Prentice–Hall, Englewood Cliffs (N.J.), 1981.

Gardner, M., "Some Packing Problems that cannot be Solved by Sitting on the Suitcase", *Scientific American*, Oct. 1979.

Garey, M.R. and Johnson, D.S., *Computers and Intractability: A Guide to the Theory of NP-Completeness*, Freeman, New York, 1979.

Geoffrion, A.M., "Lagrangian Relaxation for Integer Programming", *Mathematical Programming Study*, 2 (1974), 82-114.

Gershkoff, I., "Optimizing Flight Crew Schedules", *Interfaces*, 19 (1989), 29-43.

Gill, P.E., Murray, W. and Wright, M.H., *Practical Optimization*, Academic Press, London, 1981.

Graves, G., McBride R.D., Gershkoff, I., Anderson D., and Mahidhara, D., "Flight Crew Scheduling", *Management Science*, 39 (1993), 736-745.

Green, P.E., "Hybrid Models for Conjoint Analysis: An Expository Review", *Journal of Marketing Research*, 21 (1984), 155-169.

Green, P.E. and Krieger, A.M., "Models and Heuristics for Product Line Selection", *Marketing Science*, 4 (1985), 1-19.

Green, P.E. and Krieger, A.M., "An Application of a Product Positioning Model to Pharmaceutical Products", *Marketing Science*, 11 (1992), 117-132.

Guiltinan, J.P., "The Price Bundling of Services: A Normative Framework", *Journal of Marketing*, 51 (1987), 74-85.

Gumbel, E.J., *The Statistics of Extremes*, John Wiley & Sons, New York, 1958.

Hanson, W.A. and Martin, R.K., "Optimal Bundle Pricing", *Management Science*, 36 (1991), 155-174.

Hanson, W.A. and Martin, R.K., "Optimizing Multinomial Logit Profit Functions", Graduate School of Business, University of Chicago, 1994.

Hodgson, T.J., "A Combined Approach to the Pallet Loading Problem", *IIE Transactions*, 14 (1982), 175-182.

Hoffman, K. and Padberg, M., "Solving airline crew scheduling problems by branch-and-bound", *Management Science*, 39 (1993), 657-682.

Hu, S.T., *Homotopy Theory*, Academic Press, New York, 1959.

Infanger, G., *Planning Under Uncertainty*, The Scientific Press, Boyd & Fraser Publishing Company, 1994.

Jackson, B.B., "Winning and Keeping Industrial Customers", Lexington (MA), 1985.

Kalish, S. and Nelson, P., "An Empirical Evaluation of Multiattribute Utility and Reservation Price Measurement", Purdue University Working Paper, 1988.

Kamakura, W. and Russell, G., "A Probablistic Choice Model for Market Segmentation and Elasticity Structure", *Journal of Marketing Research*, 26 (1989), 379-390.

Khumawala, B. M., "An Efficient Branch and Bound Algorithm for the Warehouse Location Problem", *Management Science*, 18 (1972), 718-731.

Kohli, R. and Krishnamurti, R., "A Heuristic Approach to Product Design", *Management Science*, 33 (1987), 1123-33.

Kohli, R. and Sukumar, R., "Heuristics for Product–Line Design Using Conjoint Analysis", *Management Science*, 36 (1990), 1464-1478.

Lancaster, K., "The Economics of Product Variety: A Survey", *Marketing Science*, 9 (1990), 189-206.

Lewbel, A., "Bundling of Substitutes", *International Journal of Industrial Organization*, 3 (1985), 101-107.

Lorie, J. and Savage, L.J., "Three Problems in Capital Rationing", *Journal of Business*, 28 (1955), 229-239.

Louvière, J. and Woodworth, G., "Design and Analysis of Simulated Consumer Choice or Allocation Experiments: An Approach Based on Aggregate Data", *Journal of Marketing Research*, 20 (1983), 340-367.

Manski, C., "Maximum Score Estimation of the Stochastic Utility Model of Choice", *Journal of Econometrics*, 3 (1975), 205-228.

Martello, S. and Toth, P., "Optimal and Canonical Solutions of the Change Making problem", *European Journal of Operational Research*, 1 (1980), 169-175.

Martello, S. and Toth, P., *Knapsack Problems: Algorithms and Computer Implementations*, Wiley Interscience Series in Discrete Maths and Optimization, 1990.

142

McAfee, R.P., McMillan, J. and Whinston, M.D., "Multiproduct Monopoly, Commodity Bundling, and Correlation of Values", *The Quarterly Journal of Economics*, 104 (1989), 371-383.

McBride, R.D. and Zufryden, F.S., "An Integer Programming Approach to the Optimal Product Line Selection Problem", *Marketing Science*, 7 (1988), 126-140.

McFadden, D., "Conditional Logit Analysis of Quantal Choice Behavior", *Frontiers in Econometrics*, (P. Zarembka ed.), Academic Press, New York, 1974.

McFadden, D., "Econometric Models for Probabilistic Choice Among Products", *Journal of Business*, 53 (1980), 13-34.

McFadden, D., "The Choice Theory Approach to Market Research", *Marketing Science*, 5 (1986), 275-297.

Nagle, M., *The Strategy and Tactics of Pricing*, Prentice–Hall, Englewood Cliffs (N.J.), 1987.

Nahmias, S., *Production and Operations Analysis*, 2nd Edition, Irwin, Homewood (IL), 1989.

Nemhauser, G.L. and Wolsey, L.A., *Integer and Combinatorial Optimization*, Wiley Interscience Series in Discrete Mathematics and Optimization, 1988.

Ogawa, K., "An Approach to Simultaneous Estimation and Segmentation in Conjoint Analysis", *Marketing Science*, 6 (1987), 66-81.

Ong, N., "Activity–based Cost Tables to Support Wire Harness Design", *International Journal of Production Economics*, 29 (1993), 271-289.

Palfrey, T.R., "Bundling Decisions by a Multiproduct Monopolist with Incomplete Information", *Econometrica*, 51 (1983), 463-483.

Pnevmaticos, S.M. and Mann, S.H., "Dynamic Programming in Tree Bucking", *Forest Production Journal*, 22 (1973), 26-30.

Pontrajagin, L.S., *Grundzuege der kombinatorischen Topologie*, Deutscher Verlag der Wissenschaften, Berlin, 1956.

Porter, M.E., "Competitive Advantage: Creating and Sustaining Superior Performance", The Free Press, New York, 1985.

Ram, B., "The Pallet Loading Problem: A Survey", *International Journal of Production Economics*, 28 (1992), 217-225.

Rosen, J.B., "The Gradient Projection Method for Nonlinear Programming, Part I, Linear Constraints", *SIAM Journal of Applied Mathmatics*, 8 (1960), 181-217.

Rosen, J.B., "The Gradient Projection Method for Nonlinear Programming, Part II, Nonlinear Constraints", *SIAM Journal of Applied Mathmatics*, 9 (1961), 514-532.

Schmalensee, R., "Commodity Bundling by Single-Product Monopolies", *Journal of Law and Economics*, 25 (1982), 67-71.

Schmalensee, R., "Gaussian Demand and Commodity Bundling", *Journal of Business*, 57 (1984), 211-230.

Schrage, L. "Implicit Representation of Variable Upper Bounds in Linear Programming", *Mathematical Programming Study*, 4 (1975), 118-132.

Schrage, L. *User's Manual for Linear, Integer and Quadratic Programming with LINDO*, The Scientific Press, San Francisco, CA, 1989.

Schubert, H., *Topologie*, Teubner Verlag, Stuttgart, 1969.

Simon, H., *Preismanagement*, Gabler Verlag, Wiesbaden, 1992.

Simon, H., "Preisbündelung", *Zeitschrift für Betriebswirtschaft*, 62 (1992), 1213-1235.

Singh, D.K., "SPC in the Automotive Wire Harness Industry", *Industrial Engineering*, 19 (1987), 42-43.

Sobel, R., *IBM–Colossus in Transition*, New York, 1981.

Stange, K., *Angewandte Statistik*, Erster und Zweiter Teil, Springer–Verlag, Berlin, 1970/71.

Stigler, G.J., "United States vs. Loew's Inc.: A Note on Block Booking", *The Supreme Court Review*, 152 (1963), 152-157.

Stigler, G.J., "A Note On Block Booking", *The Organization of Industry*, (G.J. Stigler ed.), Irwin, Homewood (IL), 1968.

Sweeney, P.E. and Paternoster, E.R., "Cutting and Packing Problems: A Categorized Application-Oriented Research Bibliography", *Journal of the Operational Research Society*, 43 (1992), 691-706.

Telser, L.G., "Abuse in Trade Practices: An Economic Analysis", *Law and Contemporary Problems*, 30 (1965), 488-505.

Telser, L.G., "A Theory of Monopoly of Complementary Goods", *Journal of Business*, 52 (1979), 211-230.

Thompson, G.M., "Shift Scheduling in Services When Employees Have Limited Availability: An LP Approach", *Journal of Operations Management*, 9 (1990), 352-370.

Ullman, J.D., "Complexity of Sequencing Problems", *Computer and Job Scheduling Theory*, (E.G. Coffman ed.), John Wiley & Sons, New York, 1976, Chapter 4.

Ulrich, K., "The Role of Product Architecture in the Manufacturing Firm", MIT Working Paper, August 1993, forthcoming in *Research Policy*.

Vohra, R.V., "A Quick Heuristic for some Cyclic Staff Problems with Breaks", *Journal of the Operational Research Society*, 39 (1988), 1057-1061.

Warhit, E., "The Economics of Tie-in Sales", *Atlantic Economic Journal*, 8 (1980), 81-88.

Watson, T.J. Jr., "Father, Son & Co.: My Life at IBM and Beyond", Bantam Books, New York, 1990.

Wee, T.S. and Magazine, M.J., "Assembly Line Balancing as Generalized Bin-Packing", *Operations Research Letters*, 56-58.

Wilson, L.O., Weiss, A.M. and John, G., "Unbundling of Industrial Systems", *Journal of Marketing Research*, 27 (1990), 123-138.

Winston, W. L., "Operations Research: Applications and Algorithms", Duxbury Press, Belmont (CA), 1994, 476-477.

Yadav, M.S. and Monroe, K.B., "How Buyers Perceive Savings in a Bundle Price: An Examination of a Bundle's Transaction Value", *Journal of Marketing Research*, 30 (1993), 350-358.

Yosida, K., *Functional Analysis*, Springer Verlag, Berlin, 1965.

Zufryden, F.S., "A Conjoint-Measurement-Based Approach for Optimal New Product Design and Product Positioning", *Analytical Approaches to Product and Market Planning*, (A.D.Shocker ed.), Marketing Science Institute, Cambridge (MA), 1977, 100-114.

Zufryden, F.S., "Product Line Optimization by Integer Programming", Proc. Annual Meetings of ORSA/TIMS, San Diego (CA), 1982.

DUV DeutscherUniversitätsVerlag
GABLER·VIEWEG·WESTDEUTSCHER VERLAG

Aus unserem Programm

Alexander Bradel
Industriebetrieb und Verkehrsproblematik
Industrielle Maßnahmen zur Verringerung, Verlagerung und Verbesserung
des Güter- und Personenverkehrs
1995. XXVII, 336 Seiten,
Broschur DM 118,-/ ÖS 873,-/ SFr 111,-
GABLER EDITION WISSENSCHAFT
ISBN 3-8244-6223-0
Industriebetriebe sind wichtige Verkehrsverursacher und werden gleichzeitig
in wachsendem Maß von der Verkehrsproblematik negativ tangiert. Diese
Thematik wird in dieser Arbeit erstmals systematisch aus betriebswirtschaftli-
cher Sicht untersucht.

Torsten Eistert
EDI Adoption and Diffusion
International Comparative Analysis of the Automotive and Retail Industries
1996. XXI, 297 Seiten,
Broschur DM 98,-/ ÖS 725,-/ SFr 92,-
GABLER EDITION WISSENSCHAFT
"Informationsmanagement und Computer Aided Team",
hrsg. von Prof. Dr. Helmut Krcmar
ISBN 3-8244-6265-6
In spite of the benefits attributed to the electronic exchange of information
between companies the diffusion of EDI has fallen short of the prognoses. In
four case studies of EDI projects in Germany and Spain the author confronts
expectations and reality.

Volker Eßmann
Planung potentialgerechter Produkte
Ein Beitrag zur Produktkonversion
1995. XII, 156 Seiten,
Broschur DM 89,-/ ÖS 694,-/ SFr 89,-
GABLER EDITION WISSENSCHAFT
ISBN 3-8244-6130-7
Industrieunternehmen stehen vor dem Problem, neue Produkte für nicht oder
nur unzureichend ausgelastete Kapazitäten finden zu müssen, um absatz-
schwache Erzeugnisse zu ersetzen. Das Buch zeigt systematische Wege zu
einer solchen Produktkonversion.

DUV DeutscherUniversitätsVerlag
GABLER·VIEWEG·WESTDEUTSCHER VERLAG

Jörg Freiling
Die Abhängigkeit der Zulieferer
Ein strategisches Problem
1995. XX, 402 Seiten, Broschur DM 118,-/ ÖS 921,-/ SFr 118,-
GABLER EDITION WISSENSCHAFT
ISBN 3-8244-6210-9
Der Autor entwickelt strategische Optionen, die der Existenzsicherung der
Zulieferunternehmung dienen. Er geht auf die Kompensationsstrategie ein,
die sich als vielversprechend erweist, und beschreibt detailliert ihre Umset-
zung.

Astrid Hirsch
Die Betriebsstatistik in Plan- und Marktwirtschaft
Systematisierung und vergleichende Aussagen zur ehemaligen DDR und zur
Bundesrepublik Deutschland
1996. L, 559 Seiten, 104 Abb., 54 Tab.,
Broschur DM 138,-/ ÖS 1.021,-/ SFr 130,-
ISBN 3-8244-0285-8
Die Arbeit vermittelt Hinweise, ob Defekte des planwirtschaftlichen Systems
auch mit betriebsstatistischen Methoden erkannt werden konnten und ob
dortige Analysemethoden auch für die marktwirtschaftliche Betriebsstatistik
sinnvoll sind.

Holger Püchert
Ein Ansatz zur strategischen Planung von Kreislaufwirtschaftssystemen
Dargestellt für das Altautorecycling und die Eisen- und Stahlindustrie
1996. XXIII, 221 Seiten, Broschur DM 89,-/ ÖS 659,-/ SFr 84,-
GABLER EDITION WISSENSCHAFT
ISBN 3-8244-6305-9
Durch das Kreislaufwirtschafts- und Abfallgesetz entstehen für Industrie, Wirt-
schaft und genehmigende Behörden vielfältige neue Anforderungen. Dieses
Buch untersucht die rechtlichen, technischen und ökonomischen Aspekte.

Erich J. Schwarz
Unternehmensnetzwerke im Recycling-Bereich
1994. XIII, 210 Seiten,
Broschur DM 89,-/ ÖS 694,-/ SFr 89,-
GABLER EDITION WISSENSCHAFT
ISBN 3-8244-6093-9
Das zwischenbetriebliche Recycling stellt ein Instrument der betrieblichen
Umweltpolitik dar. Hieraus können industrielle Verwertungsnetze entstehen.
Im Zentrum der Untersuchung stehen Erfolgskriterien dieser umweltpoliti-
schen Instrumente.

DUV DeutscherUniversitätsVerlag

GABLER·VIEWEG·WESTDEUTSCHER VERLAG

Urban Uttenweiler
Die Wirtschaftlichkeit von Gruppenarbeit in der Automobilproduktion
Fallstudie in einer Automobilendmontage
1995. XX, 173 Seiten, 42 Abb.,
Broschur DM 89,-/ ÖS 694,-/ SFr 89,-
ISBN 3-8244-0242-4
In dieser Arbeit wird an einem konkreten Fall untersucht, wie sich die Umstellung auf Gruppenarbeit auf die Wirtschaftlichkeit ausgewirkt hat. Dabei zeigt sich, daß die Personalkosten in der Endmontage nach Einführung von Gruppenarbeit gesunken sind.

Heiko Wolters
Modul- und Systembeschaffung in der Automobilindustrie
Gestaltung der Kooperation zwischen europäischen Hersteller- und Zuliefer unternehmen
1995. XVIII, 296 Seiten,
Broschur DM 98,-/ ÖS 725,-/ SFr 92,-
GABLER EDITION WISSENSCHAFT
ISBN 3-8244-6244-3
Heiko Wolters zeigt, wie durch die Beschaffung von kompletten, funktionalen Baugruppen die Wertschöpfungskette optimiert und Kosten nachhaltig reduziert werden können.

Jens Wonigeit
Total Quality Management
Grundzüge und Effizienzanalyse
2. Auflage 1996. XXI, 265 Seiten, 28 Abb., 16 Tab.,
Broschur DM 98,-/ ÖS 765,-/ SFr 98,-
ISBN 3-8244-0287-4
In seiner Untersuchung weist der Autor unter Verwendung von empirischem Datenmaterial nach, daß Total Quality Management (TQM) tendenziell geeignet ist, Kosteneffizienz und Qualitätsproduktion gleichzeitig zu realisieren.

Die Bücher erhalten Sie in Ihrer Buchhandlung!
Unser Verlagsverzeichnis können Sie anfordern bei:

Deutscher Universitäts-Verlag
Postfach 30 09 44
51338 Leverkusen

MIX
Papier aus verantwortungsvollen Quellen
Paper from responsible sources
FSC® C105338

If you have any concerns about our products,
you can contact us on
ProductSafety@springernature.com

In case Publisher is established outside the EU,
the EU authorized representative is:
Springer Nature Customer Service Center GmbH
Europaplatz 3, 69115 Heidelberg, Germany

Printed by Libri Plureos GmbH
in Hamburg, Germany